The craft of
hand spinning

The craft of
hand spinning

Eileen Chadwick

B T Batsford Ltd London

To my Mother and Marjorie
for all their patience, help and understanding
my love and thanks.

The frontispiece shows an early example of an elegant
boudoir flax wheel with a pear-shaped cage distaff
(courtesy of the Victoria and Albert Museum)

© Eileen Chadwick 1980
First published 1980
First published in paperback 1981

ISBN 0 7134 1012 4 (paperback)

Filmset in 'Monophoto' Bembo by
Servis Filmsetting Limited, Manchester

Printed in Great Britain by
The Anchor Press Limited, Tiptree,
for the publishers B T Batsford Limited
4 Fitzhardinge Street, London W1H 0AH

Contents

Acknowledgment

This book has come together due to the generosity of many friends and the kind co-operation of the various organisations whom I have approached. Those who have encouraged and helped are too numerous to record but I extend my sincere thanks to them all.

Special gratitude goes to Theo Moorman who 'paved the way' and gave unstinting encouragement; to the late Bernard Leach for allowing the quotations heading each section to be reproduced; to Kit Houghton for the bulk of the photography; Ian Robson and S J Barrett for their part in this field; and to the following for loans of equipment, information or photographs: Phoebe Allen, Patricia Baines, Patricia Battye, Gerald Carter, Bailey Churcher, Mark Davis, the late Gladys Dickinson, Sylvia Hayes, Anne Lander, Dorothy Luke, D Paterson, Lois Pulford, Penelope Porter, Audrey Smith, Peter Teal, the late Violetta Thurston. Not least to all who were prepared to *be* photographed and gave up their time to this end, many thanks are due.

Industrial research and educational organisations have also been forthcoming in their assistance, and I am grateful to the following for their kind response: British Wool Marketing Board, CoSIRA, CIBA Review, International Wool Secretariat, Lambeg Industrial Research Association, Victoria and Albert Museum (for the frontispiece and figs 130 and 131), WIRA, the Science Museum (for figs 120, 121), and the Society of Border Leicester Sheep Breeders (for figs 10 and 11).

Introduction

Every piece of Craftwork should be an adventure

Ethel Mairet

Throughout time man has had the natural instinct, impulse and need to create. Without doing so he and those dependent on him could not have survived. Today we live in a world where mechanisation has largely taken over the production of the everyday needs of the individual in the economically advanced countries. It has also succeeded in depriving the majority of people of the satisfaction and sense of achievement derived in the making of tools, utensils and garments for everyday use.

There have always been the few who have been able to fulfil this creative urge, either as a way of life, as a craftsman in one field or another, or in a purely experimental capacity when the spirit moved them, but it is only during the last decade or two that a fundamental change has come into being. People are becoming increasingly aware of a need (subconsciously maybe) to express themselves, and in doing so to face better the stresses and changing values which are taking over all around them. So they turn to the potter's wheel, the spinner's wheel, the loom, the lacemaker's pillow, and the metalworker's and woodcarver's tools.

This urge is both infectious and exhilarating, and knows few barriers of class or nationality or culture. These people are not moving back in time, nor escaping the realities of today – they are instead recreating the right values for our present day, and should be encouraged in every way.

It is not always possible to obtain sufficient instruction and encouragement when launching into a new skill, and it may be needful to fall back on a book of reference. Perhaps, even so, too many books are written about the crafts at the present time – so much of 'how to do it'. This book may add to the list, but it is intended to reach both the beginner and those wishing to explore much further, embracing most aspects of the subject.

Without the inclusion of a complete chapter on the historical background of spinning, the contents of the book would be both unbalanced and incomplete. One might expect to find this chapter at the beginning, a fitting introduction to one of the earliest, most vital, and long lived crafts in the history of man. Yet it appears to me that it is not until one has practised the craft and become familiar with the terms used, that one can comprehend and appreciate the beauty of the ancient tools, and the evolution of the methods and equipment used.

Moreover I wish above all to encourage the beginner, from the outset, to take the tool and the raw material in his or her hands, and to spin immediately. Therefore, with this in mind, I have launched the spinner straight into some practical exercises, describing the basic processes in the most simplified form, in order to bring the aspiring spinner and his or her tools together, in action, at the earliest possible moment. Some sort of a thread is bound to result, and this is a moment of triumph. This early act of creativity is still uncluttered with the technicalities and elaborations which become so important at a later stage.

The more experienced spinner often takes on an individual approach, and some will come to favour a particular aspect of the craft, possibly developing his or her skill to great perfection in the use of a fibre other than wool, as for example mohair, silk, flax or cotton. Others will have differing motives for pursuing their interest in spinning. Experienced knitters and crocheters who have sufficient leisure time in which to spin the raw materials will find it economically advantageous to produce their own yarns, and will find that the finished product is more beautiful and durable than its commercial counterpart.

The use of vegetable dyes on hand spun yarn is also more rewarding and attractive than on most commercial yarns, and both knitters and weavers have never ending opportunities of exploration in this combination. The extremely important subject of 'finishing' processes is also discussed in some detail, both at the skein stage, in many different fibres, and also in the resultant fabric, whether the subsequent process is in weave, knit or crochet. This aspect is all too often neglected or misunderstood, and much disappointment experienced by amateur spinners can be averted if this problem can be overcome.

Finally, it is hoped that this book will help the beginner acquire all the necessary skills for producing good quality hand spun yarn, and that it will also inspire experienced spinners to experiment with different fibres and techniques, and thus take full advantage of the creative potential which this traditional craft has to offer.

1 *Overleaf* A professional hand spinner at work in her studio – in the background are a floor loom and, on the wall, fleece samples for working reference. A left hand action is being employed, with extended drafting direct from the fleece.

Part I
Spinning with wool

Procedures must be natural.
Nature's simplicity hides
a greater complexity than man's.

From *The Unknown Craftsman* by Soetsu Yanagi

1 *The basic principles of hand spinning*

The formation of yarn

Thread is formed by the combination of the twisting and drawing out of fibres in a continuous line. This can be at once achieved in its *simplest* form by taking a handful of fleece, separating the fibres from each other (by a process known as *teasing*), and then holding the mass in the left hand, drawing a few fibres between the thumb and finger of the right hand and rolling them in one direction, thereby inserting *twist*. The result is a short length of spun yarn attached to the mass of fleece. This is known as finger spinning and is a slow process, but it has been used in various parts of the world; sometimes it is used in combination with knitting, and the short length produced is immediately turned into several knitted stitches.

The simplest aid to the process of drawing out (*drafting*) and twisting is a small stick (*shaft*)

2 Various types of spindles (from left to right): hand-whittled drop spindle and distaff; modern drop spindle; ancient flax spindle with a stone whorl; a wooden toy wheel whorl with a bamboo shaft, hollowed out and cut at the top; Chinese spindle with detached crosspieces; large spindle, shaft and whorl; hip spindle; spindle made from the stripped top of a Spruce tree; cotton spindle and support bowl

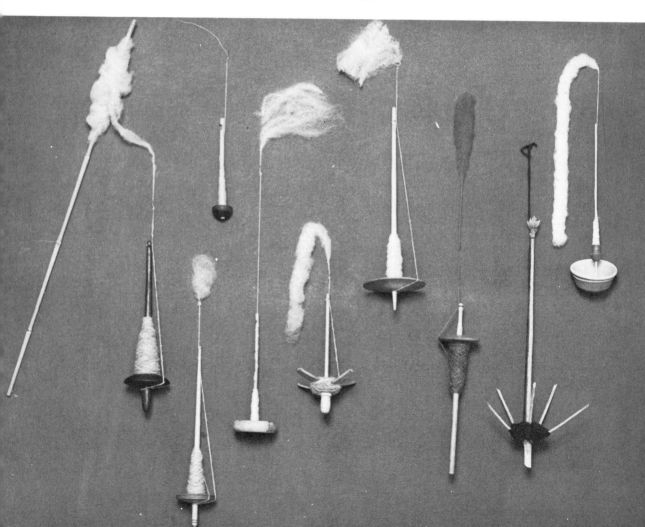

weighted at one end (*whorl*), either twirled in the palm of the hand, or suspended and twisted, or supported in a bowl and spun like a top. The stick or spindle itself serves as a 'bobbin' on which to wind the resultant thread as it is produced (figure 2).

The more elaborate spinning apparatus, as in the case of the spindle wheel (Great wheel), flyer wheel (figure 3), spinning jenny or modern spinning machinery (and there are many types), are all designed to produce yarn using one or other method of *draft*, *twist* and *wind on*.

The initial preparation of the fibre has a crucial bearing on the character of the resultant yarn, as will be appreciated when this is dealt with in detail later. To express it in simple terms, fibres can (1) be opened out from the dense mass and then aligned by a *combing* process,

and finally spun to retain the fibre alignment in the direction of the yarn flow, or (2) they can be opened out and prepared in such a way (i.e. *carded*) that the fibres are drafted into the yarn to lie in all directions, thus producing a comparatively air-filled thread.

Yarn can be spun in varying degrees of twist and in a range of thicknesses (*counts*) from very heavy to gossamer fine, the procedure being in each case essentially that of draft, twist, and wind on. The following two sections constitute a simple introduction to the principles involved in spinning with a drop spindle and a spinning wheel.

3 A range of modern wheels (from left to right): Norwegian upright wheel, Shetland wheel, Great wheel, two-band Norwegian (Saxony) wheel; the three spinning wheels in the foreground are flyer wheels, the (Great) wheel in the background is a spindle wheel

Using a drop spindle

A simple drop (suspended) spindle can be made from a straight twig cut from the hedgerow, or from a piece of narrow dowelling. Choose a stick of pencil thickness, and about 10 in (25 cm) long. Whittle one end to a point and cut a notch near the top of the other end, then drive the pointed end through a round medium-sized potato or wooden toy wheel.

Tie a length of strong woollen yarn firmly onto the shaft near the base of the spindle,

hitch it once round the underside of the base or whorl (i.e. the potato), then loop it into the notch at the top, allowing about 12 in (20 cm) of thread upwards beyond this point.

Take a lock of fleece, separate the fibres slightly to prevent them from clinging together too firmly and thus obstructing movement in spinning, and overlap this lock with the end of the thread, holding them both in the left hand, and allowing the spindle to hang free. With the right hand twist the spindle in a clockwise direction, grasping the top and giving it a sharp flick, and immediately draw

4 Spindle spinning direct from the fleece: drawing down the fibres

5 Twisting the yarn

down a few of the fibres from the lock to cover thinly the last 2 in (5 cm) of the thread. Twist again and draw out the lock between the fingers and thumbs of each hand and then allow twist to run up onto these few fibres by releasing the hold of the lower hand (right hand), thus making a short length of spun yarn.

Repeat this twisting of the spindle and drawing out of the lock several times (taking care that the spindle does not go into reverse). Unhitch the thread, then wind it onto the shaft near the whorl by holding it taut and horizontal in the left hand, and twirling the spindle round, altering the angle frequently in order to build up the yarn in an even distribution near the whorl end of the shaft. Re-hitch the newly spun thread onto the notch, allowing about 8 in (20 cm) of yarn between the top of the spindle and the lock of fleece. Continue this twisting, drafting and winding process. (See figures 4 and 5, and also figure 58.)

If insufficient twist is allowed, the yarn will lack strength and therefore break. If excessive twist occurs before drafting, too many fibres will be held together and the resulting thread will be too thick.

Using a spinning wheel

Check that the wheel is ready for use. Attach a 24 in (60 cm) length of strong woollen thread firmly onto the bobbin shaft, hitch it over the first hook on the flyer and thread it through the orifice (i.e. the hole in the spindle shaft). Holding the end of the thread and a lock of unprepared fleece between finger and thumb of the right hand, use the left hand to set the wheel in motion, and whilst treadling, draw with the same hand several fibres from the lock forward onto the twisting thread to effect the join.

Continue to draft a group of fibres from the lock between the two hands by a short forward motion of the left hand, and then allowing the twist to run up towards the right hand. This action should be repeated continuously whilst the wheel turns at a modest speed. At

intervals it becomes necessary to move the thread onto the next hook of the flyer to allow a gradual build up of the spun yarn evenly across the length of the bobbin shaft.

Care must be taken not to let twist run up into the lock beyond the left hand hold, nor must too much or too little twist be inserted into the spun thread before it is allowed to run in through the orifice and onto the flyer. This can be partially controlled by altering the tension on the drive band, though the main control is through the hands.

As the spinner uses up a lock, another one should be overlapped onto the remaining portion of the one in use, and the process continued.

A very satisfactory thread can be produced by this method, and it is a simple way to start, provided the locks are in easy working condition – namely that they are sufficiently 'open' to allow the fibres to move freely. In every spinning process there is a sliding and overlapping action of the fibres upon each other. It is therefore desirable when possible, to use fleece that has been recently sheared, as then the natural oil is still fluid.

Should the beginner find difficulty in co-ordinating hands and foot at this stage, it can be helpful to elicit the assistance of someone able to treadle the wheel evenly and smoothly at a moderate to slow speed, thus allowing total concentration on the part of the spinner in the production of the yarn.

When using a wheel for the first time it is desirable to spend some time treadling, (making sure that the whole of the foot is on the treadle, and the wheel turns consistently in the same direction), without making any attempt at producing a thread. Eventually it becomes a simple matter to look around, think of other matters and relax one's body whilst treadling smoothly, either fast or slowly, without effort. When this point is reached it should be a comparatively easy matter to co-ordinate hand movements with treadling, and spin without assistance, particularly if a certain modicum of skill has already been achieved in the use of the drop spindle.

2 *Designing the yarn*

The first chapter showed how a thread can be produced in the most simple and basic way, and the use of a good medium staple and open fleece for this purpose is an excellent introduction to the art of spinning because it overcomes, in the minimum of time, the initial difficulties. However this is only a beginning, and it is essential to have a fuller understanding of the whole process as applied to wool before one can achieve professional results. Let it be said here that one's first crude, uneven efforts at spinning need not necessarily be despised and thrown away. Provided it is not disastrously overspun, a thread can be dyed, and subsequently knitted or woven to produce an attractive and unique piece. This should stir one to more ambitious results, and a better understanding of the nature and behaviour of hand spun yarn in use.

Before launching on a spinning programme, it is necessary to consider a number of important points, since many different factors affect the appearance and behaviour of the yarn. The points to bear in mind are as follows:

1 The end product – whether it is designed for weaving, knitting, crochet or embroidery.

2 The choice of fleece – its suitability for the purpose intended in behaviour and characteristics.

3 The type of spin – woollen or worsted, or a variation of these.

4 The type of yarn – singles or plied, high twist or low twist, direction of twist, fineness or thickness.

5 The type of finishing process to be used – wet finishing, tentering, blocking, steaming etc.

6 Wheel spinning direct from the fleece: locks of fleece stand ready in the basket on the floor, (the basket above contains Shetland rolags)

The end product

There are many who think only in terms of weaving, others are confirmed knitters or crocheters. Each will need to design their yarn in relation to the character of the finished article they intend to produce. A rough estimate of the overall weight of yarn required will be desirable, and this in turn requires great care in the choice of fleece.

The choice of fleece

There are endless varieties and qualities of fleece available to the handspinner, and some experience is needed before a spinner is able to recognise the qualities that are necessary for different end products. Differing fleece types have different characteristics – for example, some have high felting potential, while some are exceptionally light and springy. Laundering of the finished article and friction in wear react differently on different fleece types. Some are smooth and lustrous whilst others may be wiry or harsh. Between these widely differing types there are many that are eminently suitable for spinning purposes.

The type of spin

Spinning techniques for wool can be divided into two main types: woollen spin and worsted spin. In the former, the (carded) fibres are rolled (to form a rolag) in a direction not aligned to that of the resulting yarn and this produces a spongy, air-filled thread. In the latter, the (combed) fibres are aligned to flow directionally into the yarn, to form a smoother, more solid thread. Woollen yarn is therefore lighter in weight (per yardage) and warmer in feel due to the still air content held within it. Each has its own ideal use, and the aspiring hand spinner should practise the skills required for each type of spin.

8 This hand knitted shawl is 5 feet (1.5 m) square and weighs 7 ounces (200 g); 300 yards (274 m) of 2 ply yarn were required for each ounce (28 g), and the fleeces used were Soay, St Kilda, Shetland, Mank Loughton and Portland

When the fleece has been selected, the type of spin suitable for the wool must be considered very carefully. Some long-stapled lustre types would probably not spin a satisfactory woollen yarn. A yarn to be spun as a worsted would almost invariably be plied, while a short-stapled, high crimp, spongy fleece would require a woollen spin or semi-worsted, and would probably not be plied.

Spinning techniques

Throughout this book, the following terms are used to differentiate between the various subdivisions of spinning techniques (each of these techniques is explained more fully in chapter 6):

1 *Woollen* – spun from a rolag using the long draw technique.

2 *Semi-woollen* – spun from a rolag using a short drafting technique (this is not a generally accepted term but it is used here to differen-

7 Spindle spun yarn from a Jacobs fleece has here been worked into a crocheted waistcoat

tiate between drafted woollen and a semi-worsted).

3 *Semi-worsted* – spun from a lock or direct from the fleece, using a short drafting action.

4 *Worsted type* – spun on the left-hand side when using a wheel, using combed locks of uniform fibre length and aligning the fibres completely to the yarn direction, and a short drafting action (again not a universally used term but employed here to make a clear distinction between this method and that of the true worsted).

5 *True worsted* – spun from elaborately processed tops, which have been prepared using a pair of heated wool combs, and a pad and diz, and spun on the left of the wheel. The fibres are aligned to the yarn direction in a short drafting action, with relatively high twist, and subsequently doubled (plied).

Note that the terms *thread* and *yarn* are often interchangeable. The terms *twist* and *spin* also have a similar connotation at times.

The type of yarn
Singles and plied yarns

If the yarn is required for knitting or crocheting, it is desirable to ply it, though there are exceptions; a 2 ply tends to produce more character than that of a 3 ply. Variations in size of plied yarns can be produced by the size, i.e. thickness or thinness, of the singles yarn. A woollen spun yarn is more bulky in character than a worsted in relation to the number of overlapping fibres in a given length, and in consequence the plied woollen yarn will also appear thicker to the eye though the weight will be less.

A singles yarn is more widely used in weaving except in the case of a true worsted, which is plied. For instance, tweed type fabrics are normally composed of singles yarns in both warp and weft, as are many other woollen fabrics. Combinations of the two, i.e. singles and plied, can be used to create textural effects. The permutations and combinations in this field cannot be enumerated, but some suggestions and examples will be touched on in chapter 7. Spinning of extremely fine yarns and extra bulky yarns, together with the special methods used to effect these qualities, are also described in chapter 8.

High twist and low twist yarns

Twist has an important bearing on the finished product. There are a number of factors to consider. When two singles yarns are twisted together to form a plied yarn, the spindle which twists the two together will normally be rotated in the opposite direction to that which was used for the singles. In the plying process some initial twist will be lost in each singles yarn and this has to be allowed for in the initial spinning. On rare occasions a lightly spun singles can be plied by continuing to use the same direction of twist in the plying (doubling) process, but this is uncommon and produces a totally different effect.

A high twist singles yarn used throughout a woven fabric will naturally produce a crisper cloth and a clearer weave structure than that similarly woven in a lightly twisted yarn. Moreover the fabric will be liable to less creasing. It may also resist the degree of felting that would occur freely in one composed of less twisted yarn.

Medium to low twist yarns of the same fleece and similar yardage will naturally be comparatively soft and air-filled, and consequently weigh less. In other words one specific weight of the lesser twist yarn will carry more length than the high twist, and have a different character. In addition to this the type of spin (woollen, worsted or one of the several semi-worsteds) will have a bearing on its character.

Direction of twist

Twist is imposed on a group of overlapping fibres by the turning of a spindle, be it by hand, or through the instrument of a wheel or other mechanical device, in a clockwise or anticlockwise direction. A clockwise twist is referred to as Z twist, and an anticlockwise as S twist. If singles yarn is spun clockwise, it is normally plied anticlockwise and vice versa. There are, however, also many instances, especially in woven structures, in which opposing directions of twist are used in particular sequences for very definite effects. These can be for purely visual impact or for tactile quality, strength and durability, crease resistance, draping quality, or any other reason.

A striking example of this can be cited in the case of a crepe-type fabric, though a hand spinner can produce some of the essential assets of this type of cloth in something more substantial than is found in a commercially produced wool crepe. This is a comparatively lightweight cloth which is extremely resilient and virtually uncrushable. The weave is plain weave (or tabby) having equal numbers of warp and weft threads (ends and picks) per inch (per 2.5 cm). The yarn is fine and highly twisted, each alternate thread in both warp and weft being of an opposite direction of twist to its neighbour. This prevents a natural 'bedding' of the yarns in either direction, thus creating a springy, totally crease-resistant fabric.

Texture

For knitting or crocheting an item, it is probable that the yarn will be required to be uniform throughout. A yarn intended for embroidery may not require so much uniformity. In weaving the quantities needed are likely to be much greater than with knitting or embroidery. They may require to be uniform throughout, or, for instance, the warp may be twice as fine as the weft. In a warp-dominant, ribbed fabric, for example, the alternate warp ends could be thick and thin, and likewise so of the weft. Other fabrics could employ textured stripes or checks of thicker threads grouped and spaced across a mainly fine background to give a textured visual effect and handle, irrespective of colour. These heavier threads can remain as thick singles, but heavier plied yarns can be employed in this way too, although the result will not be quite the same.

Fine yarns

A very lightweight knitted or woven shawl will call for a very finely spun yarn. This will probably require more twist than one would normally tend to give it, and it would be advisable to produce a trial piece before embarking upon the main work. It would be valuable to carry the trial piece through all stages, including the finishing process, as dramatic changes can take place at this stage.

Factors which are contributory to the final overall effect are: *the type of fleece, type of spin, method of yarn washing, the dyeing process, the knit, crochet or weave design, and perhaps most of all, the wet finishing process.* Some types of fleece become appreciably more bulky after relaxation and washing than they appear whilst being spun, others tend to felt easily or develop a fluffy or hairy surface during the finishing process. Fineness is comparative, and must be carefully related to the product in mind, and with an awareness of the many factors involved.

Thick yarns

Thick and excessively thick yarns are often required when floor rugs are the object in mind. A wheel carrying an especially large orifice and bobbin facilitates this, e.g. an Indian Spinner or special Jumbo attachment. A spindle wheel (Great wheel) and also a drop spindle gives complete scope for any thickness, though the latter is slower in output and therefore not so practical if large quantities are required.

A suitable fleece must be chosen and a fair degree of twist is needed to give a 'clean' finish and good durability to a floor rug. It is often more desirable to spin a medium thick yarn for this purpose, and to use several yarns together in the weft. This is particularly effective if each single component is dyed a slightly different tone, giving subtlety and life to the work, which could not be similarly achieved if thick yarns were used singly. Colour and tonal blends can also be created in mixing coloured and dyed fleece when carding.

Excessively thick yarns, which are little more than hand twisted rolags, also make thick yet soft and durable rug yarns. Thick, lightly spun yarns can also be used in moderation in dress or furnishing fabrics. These are often most effective in slub or two-colour plied yarns.

Embroidery threads

Designing a thread for use in embroidery opens up a wealth of possibilities. To begin with it may be desirable to create the fabric base for embroidery application by spinning and weaving the desired cloth. The yarns to be used as embroidery threads, in any one embroidered work, may vary a great deal. For instance both animal and vegetable fibres may be combined in the creation of a thread that would be impractical for weave or knit purposes. Conversely embroiderers using commercially produced fabrics and threads may need to add only a small quantity of hand spun yarn at strategic points, as for example for use in couching. The field is wide open and brings new dimensions into this craft.

The finishing process

The finishing process in a woollen fabric is of the utmost importance and must be considered in relation to its effect on the type of fleece used, the type of yarn(s) incorporated in the fabric, and the cloth structure itself.

A woven fabric, in wool, is structurally incomplete in most cases unless it undergoes a wet finishing process. This is designed either to set it permanently in its original loom state, or conversely to cause varying degrees of shrinkage (sometimes considerable shrinkage). The wet finishing process also initially removes oil and dirt (if present) and softens the handle of the cloth. As some types of yarn and some varieties of fleece have high felting propensities, an open structured fabric composed of these would shrink dramatically and change character completely if subjected to rigorous friction action in the wet finishing process. Conversely a closely woven fabric having a high twist yarn, composed of a non-felting type fleece, would require a prolonged friction action in the wet process to give it the firm handle and durable quality required of it.

There are occasions when a steam press (or use of a damp cloth and iron) is sufficient, but a lightly spun yarn can lose its liveliness in the woven piece if too much pressure or too hot an iron is applied. The danger of this in future laundering must be considered when designing the yarn. Tentering (stretching taut until dry) of woven fabrics, blocking and steaming of knitted and crocheted fabrics, all have a bearing on the finished article, and because they have a different effect on different types of yarn, the knowledge gained by experience will assist in establishing the best choice of finishing process for the end product in mind.

3 *Breeds of sheep and fleece types*

9 Mountain and Hill sheep: Cheviot hogs gathered for shearing in a stone-walled fank at Amat, Ross-shire

Sources of supply

The British Wool Marketing Board gives detailed information on all types, qualities and characteristics of the entire fleece yield of the United Kingdom and Northern Ireland each year. (This can be obtained on application to their head office, and is primarily intended to assist farmers and wool buyers in the textile

10 Longwool and Lustre sheep: young Border Leicesters with immature coats

11 Shortwool and Down sheep: Dorset Horn

12 Longwool and Lustre sheep: a Cotswold with characteristic forelock over the eyes

13 Shortwool and Down sheep: Suffolk Down

trade.) The sheep farmers' total yield per year is termed the *clip*, and shearing normally takes place in late May and June in lowland and Southern areas, whilst in hill country and more northern areas June and July are considered more suitable. If shearing is too long delayed some breeds of sheep tend to lose part of their fleece, rubbing it off against rough surfaces such as posts, stone walls or tree trunks. The growth of new wool will also have begun.

The question of sources of supply of fleece for the hand spinner is one which can present certain problems, and it is important to know something about the types and characteristics of fleeces likely to be available and suitable. An increasing number of individuals in many countries are keeping small numbers of sheep, sometimes so few as to be able to divide up a single paddock into two or three small areas, thereby alternating their grazing areas throughout the year.

In Britain, these 'mini' sheep farmers do not require to register with the BWMB and can shear the fleeces for their own use and to offer to friends. Sheep farmers are normally registered with the BWMB, but a single fleece or two can often be obtained from a local breeder if he or she is prepared to take the trouble to allow a spinning acquaintance to select a fleece at, or soon after, shearing time. Official sources of supply are the various wool staplers scattered in centres throughout the country (who are responsible to the BWMB) and the Board itself. Some sources for suppliers of fleeces and wool *matchings* (parts of fleece of uniform quality and type) are listed at the end of the book.

When applying for a fleece, state the type required, the grade (if known), approximate weight, approximate staple length, handle, and intended use. It is advisable to send first for an application form which lists the range of fleeces available, with prices. When buying a fleece, choose a hog (first shearing yearling) if possible, in preference to a ewe or a wether. 'Pick' fleeces are always quality fleeces in whatever class.

Breeds and crossbreds
Breed classification

As far as British wools are concerned there are three main classifications (and eight official grading specifications):

1 Mountain and Hill
2 Longwool or Lustre
3 Shortwool or Down

There are approximately fifty breeds of sheep in Great Britain and many hundreds of crosses. Crossbreeding is practised for a number of reasons, but improving the quality and characteristics of the fleece is often of minor consideration. Stamina, suitability for prevalent soil and climate conditions and altitude, and size of meat cuts are the main determining factors. Nevertheless this crossbreeding produces a rich variety of fleece types, and the hand spinner who is fortunate enough to obtain the best from a range of good clips will be well served.

Origins of sheep breeds

About a million years ago wild sheep roamed the plains of India, Asia and many other parts of the world. It is thought that flocks were domesticated by the Mesopotamians some 9,000 years ago. There are three main types of primitive wild sheep originating from South Eastern Europe, mountain sheep from the Far and Middle East through Alaska and in North Africa, and those roaming through Persia, India and Tibet, whose descendants are to be found there still. All had fine curving horns, a longish coarse outer coat, and a fine soft short undercoat.

Not very much information is available on the early sheep of the British Isles, but by the Middle Ages it appears that there were several varieties well established. At the time of the great export trade in raw wool, the monasteries owned large flocks of sheep, and these were in all probability largely Cotswolds, Lincolns and Leicesters. The Scottish Blackface of the present time derives from the original short and coarse-woolled mountain type. It is now largely bred for the protective covering the fleece affords either for its water resistance in wet areas, or warmth in exposed climatic conditions. The outer hair fibres are suitable for carpets, whilst the undercoat is normally used for tweeds, and similar hard-wearing fabrics.

Today the breeds and crossbreeds are innumerable. In Britain the selection is incomparable, and nowhere else can be found such quality in every class. The hand spinner can obtain every conceivable type from the extra fine and short stapled brown undercoat of the ancient Soay breed, and the bouncy, crimpy, white fleece of the Southdown, (the wide range of Shortwool or Down breeds were developed comparatively recently), to the creamy lustrous curly coat of the large Cotswold, or the long coarse hairy variety of the Herdwick or Swaledale.

Pedigree flocks and rare breeds

There are always a number of pure bred flocks being raised, and in recent years many of the rarer breeds of ancient origin are being fostered, and flocks built up both privately and in rare breed parks. Some of these are naturally of special attraction to the hand spinner.

In Britain, the preservation of the ancient Viking breeds, such as the Soay and St Kilda sheep, which in the mid-twentieth century

had diminished to the few remaining on the island of St Kilda in the Outer Hebrides, is of major importance in the conservation of the nation's heritage. The delightful little Soay sheep yields a fine soft, short-stapled fleece which sheds naturally. In order to gather it in

14 *Above* Shortwool and Down sheep: a Shetland ewe

15 *Below* Rare breeds: (left) newly sheared Jacobs and (right) Soay; the latter are plucked rather than sheared

its best condition it must be plucked by hand, lock by lock.

There are many other breeds which were nearing extinction whose numbers are now growing due to current awareness. The ancient breed from the Isle of Man, the Manx Loughton, is now preserved in farm parks as well as on the island itself; its fleece has an attractive 'woolly' handle and a light golden brown colour. Another rare breed is the Portland, probably imported into Britain from Spain several centuries ago – it is a small animal with a soft, white fleece of short staple. The Lonk is also an ancient breed with a medium coarse staple. Not least is the increasingly popular Jacobs sheep – a very rare breed in Britain until the 1960s – which, since the instigation of the Jacobs Sheep Society, has increased in number in a most spectacular manner. Crossed with a Clun Forest, it produces an all-black or grey-black fleece of desirable quality.

Obtainable from the Shetland and Orkney islands in Scotland are the tiny soft brown fleeces of the Shetland breed that thrives there; the warm brown colour is known as moorit – other fleeces range from white and grey to fawn. Shetland sheep are also found in small flocks in suitable territory in parts of the mainland of Britain.

Amongst the Longwool lustres is the Cotswold – an early breed from the Cotswold hills of England – which is now being revived in several areas. It is a large animal with a curly, cream-coloured, highly lustrous coat, which may be difficult for the hand spinner to work, but can be extremely beautiful.

Breeds recommended for hand spinning

Though British sheep breeds are generally classified under the three main headings of Shortwool and Down, Longwool and Lustre, and Mountain and Hill, the majority of the flocks throughout the country are not pure bred. It is therefore more practical to divide the groups as shown below, and list the breeds and crosses under these headings:

1 Fairly short staple and soft handle – degree of fineness (i.e. quality count) 55–60s.

2 Medium length staple, open texture, slightly coarser – degree of fineness 48–54s.

3 Fairly long and lustrous or demi-lustrous – degree of fineness 36–48s.

4 Long staple and coarse, hairy fibres – degree of fineness 32–48.

Group I: Fairly short staple and soft handle

Breed of sheep	Average weight of fleece
Southdown Often very short stapled, exceptionally fine fibre diameter, springy but soft and spongy, not easy to spin but there is no substitute.	6 lb
Dorset Down Fairly short, dense, springy in character.	6 lb
Dorset Horn Longer staple, fine and soft and easy to handle.	6 lb
Suffolk Down A breed which is found more widely distributed than most, Suffolk crosses are extremely common. Suffolk Down crosses are especially good for hand spinning.	7 lb
Oxford Down A larger fleece with longer staple, but especially resilient and soft in handle. It is used for crossing with Downs and Lustres.	9 lb
Radnor Often very soft and fine but longer stapled, not springy. Usually good for fine knitting. Useful for crossbreeding.	5 lb
Shetland Often extremely soft and very fine. Staple length variable. White fleeces are usually the finest quality. Coloured fleeces range from dark, warm browns to buffs, greys and whites. Not always easy to use.	3 lb
Manx Loughton A very fine, soft, creamy brown fleece, with some spring	

and density. A native of the Isle of Man, and among the rare breed survivals.   4 lb

Soay   Among the rare breeds, this delightful little animal carries an exceptionally short-stapled, fine fibre which is normally plucked (rooed).   2 lb

Ryeland   A breed of ancient origin in Britain. Yields a fine soft high quality fleece of springy character.   7 lb

Clun Forest   A fairly fine dense fleece. Variable but usually easy to handle. Useful for crossbreeding.   5 lb

The fleeces in Group I require carding for woollen or semi-woollen spinning. Several can be spun direct from the fleece for semi-worsted if the fibre length allows for combing.

Group II: Medium staple and open texture

Kerry Hill   Variable, can be very silky but often inclined to be coarse.   5 lb

Jacobs   Variable. Usually soft medium length staple. Proportions of coloured areas vary from sheep to sheep.   6 lb

Welsh Mountain   Usually very open, medium length staple, medium to coarse, tweed type, often contains kemps. Black fleeces from crosses or pure breds are inclined to be coarser. Good range of greys produced from crosses.   4 lb

Lonk   Varies a great deal in quality. Suitable for knitting when not too coarse. Medium staple.   5 lb

Cheviot   A very good fleece for spinning for hardwearing fabrics. Contains a pleasant combination of resilience and a slight lustre.   5 lb

Fleeces in Group II can be carded, combed or spun from the fleece, and are suitable for woollen, semi-woollen or semi-worsted spinning.

Group III: Fairly long and lustrous or demi-lustrous

Border Leicester   Medium to coarse, longish staple. Good handle. Popular for hand spinners for worsteds or worsted type spinning.   9 lb

Border Leicester x Suffolk   A common cross with a softer shorter staple and good handle. Can be carded or combed.   8 lb

Romney Marsh   Fairly fine, medium to long staple. Very good for hand spinning especially for worsteds and worsted type.   9 lb

Wensleydale   A rather long and very curly creamy fleece, suitable for worsteds; not easy.   15 lb

Cotswolds   Long and lustrous. Among the rare breeds. Not easy, but a very attractive worsted is possible.   12 lb

Fleeces in Group III are not suitable for beginners. They should not normally be carded (exceptions are Border Leicester and Suffolk). Combing for worsted or worsted type is recommended, following careful washing.

Group IV: Long staple and coarse, hairy fibres

Herdwick   Long, fairly coarse, and sometimes kempy. Good for floor rugs or heavy furnishing fabric. Can be carded and rolled sideways or combed.   4 lb

Rough Fell   Similar to above.   5 lb

Masham   Variable, often silky, but mainly long and coarse.   6 lb

Scottish Blackface   Longer and coarser than Herdwick and not so easy to handle.   5 lb

Fleeces in Group IV are not recommended for beginners, but can be used for rough-textured floor rugs.

4 Preparing the fleece

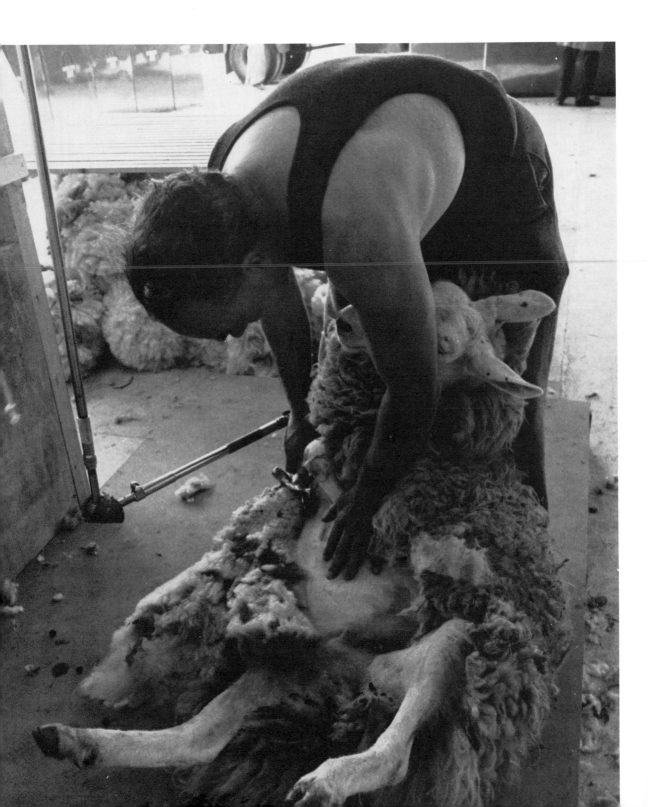

The different stages of preparing a fleece for spinning depend on the type of spin to be used. The fleece is first sorted to separate the qualities of wool. If the fleece is dirty it may be scoured (washed), and if necessary oiled. If the fibres are to be woollen spun they must first be teased, carded and rolled. If they are to be worsted spun, they may be combed, or it is possible to spin direct from the fleece. If a true worsted spin is required, the preparation and combing process is fairly elaborate, and this procedure is described in chapter 6.

Sorting

Fleece sorting is the term used to describe the dividing up of a single fleece into various fibre qualities. Careful sorting is essential if an overall uniformity is the criteria to be aimed at in the production of a piece of work. This uniformity may be arrived at in several ways.

1 A separation may be made of the different qualities present in a fleece, followed by an even blending of, say, two or more of these qualities in the carding process.

2 Similar areas (matchings) of two or more similar fleeces may be blended, as for example the head and shoulders of both.

3 If only a small quantity is required, this may be found in one area of a single fleece.

4 Overall uniformity may also be obtained through the use of one quality in warp and another in weft or in each of the singles of a 2 ply yarn.

A fleece is usually presented to the sorter rolled up in a complete package, which is capable of being tossed about without becoming un-wound. The shearer removes the fleece from the sheep in one piece (figure 16), lays it out flat, the outer side uppermost. He then folds it lengthways into three layers, and rolls it tightly from the tail end (much as one rolls up a sleeping bag). Finally he takes a piece of the head end, pulls and twists repeatedly until he has a sufficient ropelike length to reach round

16 Shearing a fleece in one piece

the rolled fleece and then tuck firmly into the end of the 'rope' that is attached to the main body of the fleece (figures 17, 18, 19, 20). The fleece sorter must therefore reverse this procedure in order to open the fleece out intact. Care must be exercised in so doing, as it is easy to part the layers incorrectly and 'lose one's way'.

Practice and experience will enable the sorter to recognise the changes in quality in the different areas of each fleece. These vary considerably from fleece to fleece so that both hand and eye must be employed to achieve this accurately. The word 'quality' refers mainly to fibre diameter, though fibre length, and amount of crimp, and particularly soundness, may also be contributory factors. Degrees of quality in a fleece are as follows.

1 *Head*
This is usually of the very finest in relation to the rest of the fleece, but in arable fed sheep especially, it often has so much foreign matter present, such as hayseeds, that it is unsatisfactory for the hand spinner to handle. It is known as *moiety*.

2 *Shoulders (or head and shoulders)*
This is the best quality, known as *extra diamond*, and in a good fleece it may be extended halfway down the flanks and across the forward part of the back.

3 *Back*
This is normally referred to as *diamond*. In poorer quality fleeces there may be no extra diamond and the diamond may be confined to shoulders and flanks.

4 *Rump*
The rump area of the back takes the worst of the weather and is frequently thinner and dryer. This area and the remainder of the flanks are termed *prime*.

5 *Belly*
A narrow strip on each edge of the shorn fleece is the belly and is often excessively short and rubbed into a felted state due to the sheep lying on it, and it is called the *picklock*.

17 *Above* Laying the fleece out flat

18 *Above* Folding the fleece into three

19 *Below* Rolling up the fleece from the tail end

20 *Below* Tying up the rolled fleece

6 *Hind legs*

The coarser fleece found down the hind legs (sometimes more like hair than fibre) is known as *britch*.

7 *Tail*

The tail area, and sometimes the belly, is frequently found to be soiled or encrusted with manure. These parts are referred to as *skirtings* and should be removed before sorting begins properly.

Method of sorting

1 Unroll and spread out the fleece onto a large table or the floor, covered with a sheet of medium or heavy gauge polythene (plastic).

2 Remove the skirtings. (These can be soaked in cold water and the liquor used in the greenhouse. Alternatively the encrusted parts can be dug into the soil or compost for its value as a plant food.)

3 Divide up the different qualities, starting with the finest, by careful feel and observation. It is sometimes found necessary to sort a fleece into five or even six qualities. Others need only four divisions, and in a very good, even fleece, only three. The areas should be separated by parting them with the hands, palms

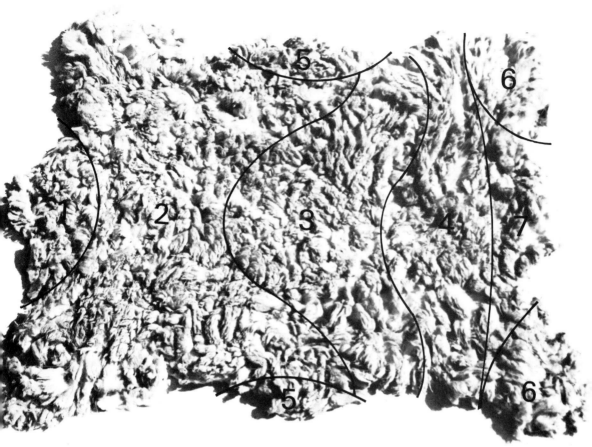

21 Sorting a fleece into qualities

downwards, following the natural parting of the locks, and pushing firmly against the table or floor surface in opposite directions.

4 When the different qualities have been divided, label each lot. They are best stored in paper or cloth bags, rather than polythene, as the latter prevents air circulation.

Fleece qualities

Fleece qualities are normally similar to that found in the same area on the correspondingly opposite side of the animal. The similar qualities in one or more fleeces is called *matchings*. It is often easiest to recognise these by drawing out locks from each area and scrutinising them thoroughly by both hand and eye. Endeavour to see fibre diameter variation, look for variation in crimp, staple length, density and general appearance. To test soundness stretch a lock taut and flick it with the finger end. A slight weakness along its length will cause fibre breakage. This weak area may show as a marked line, and is due either to illness of the animal at some point in the year, or poor feed, or drought. Do not use such a fleece.

Scouring

For the hand spinner, it is often preferable to spin direct from the unwashed fleece (or *in the grease* as it is termed) and the sooner this is possible after shearing the better, as the natural oil is fresh and free flowing, making spinning delightfully easy.

Fleece should be kept in a cool place. It should not be left spread out, as this would inevitably hasten the drying up of the natural oil. If, on the other hand, a fleece has come to be, or is at the outset, 'sticky' to handle and is inclined to cling when teased and carded, it may be desirable to wash (scour) it. *This must be done with the greatest care.* Certain types of fleece have a stronger tendency to felting than others, and if this occurs more harm may be done than if left unwashed. The best and safest method to adopt is as follows.

1 Immerse the part of the fleece intended for washing (before teasing), in a receptacle containing sufficient tepid water to cover it well.

2 Soak it for several hours or overnight.

3 Lift it out and drain. Avoid squeezing it, at any stage.

4 Prepare warm water to cover the fleece and allow for movement, and add a gentle, high quality liquid detergent which is designed for use on wool. Lissapol N (now Synperonic N, an ICI product), Teepol and Stergene are all considered suitable.

5 Immerse the fleece, and move it about very gently. Avoid agitating it, at any stage.

6 Lift it out, and allow it to drain.

7 Prepare a clear rinse at the same temperature.

8 Immerse the fleece, move it around gently, lift it out, and allow it to drain. Give it a second rinse in the same temperature, and drain again.

9 Spread it on a rack or net to dry in a moderate atmosphere. If oil is to be applied, it must be done after teasing.

Teasing

This is done prior to carding and facilitates the latter process. It entails the parting of the fibres one from another so that they can be applied to the carders in a thin or moderately thin film. The thoroughness of this opening out process is partly dependent on individual preference, and partly on the character and condition of the fleece. One in which the locks are clearly defined, but where there is no tendency to clinginess, requires only a slight opening out of each lock, and these can be applied to the carder with little disturbance to their natural alignment. Conversely a 'cotty'

(clingy) fleece, or short stapled, close textured variety will card best if the fleece is very well teased. In this case a few small locks will be transformed into a relatively sizable pile of cloudlike fibre mass. There are two methods of teasing.

First method: Maximum degree

Take a handful of the selected part of the fleece, and, whilst holding one lock of this mass within the left hand, allow a little to protrude beyond the confines of the whole length of the thumb and the tips of all the fingers. With the finger and thumb of the right hand draw the fibres out at right angles from the left hand in a progressive and repeated action, allowing an unbroken film of fibres to be released through the left hand as needed. This will lie on the floor or the spinner's lap in a loose mass (figure 22).

Second method: Minimum degree

When a minimum degree of teasing is needed, each individual lock is taken in the left hand and the tips are stroked and eased free of each other with the finger and thumb of the right hand, the root being treated similarly if required, and the locks are piled up neatly in readiness for carding. This method is also commonly used in preparation for combing.

During these teasing processes it is necessary to remove any foreign matter, such as seeds and thorns, as these will cause the fibres to cling together in the affected area. Much of the dirt and other matter will fall from the fleece during teasing – for this reason, and also due to the natural grease present in the unwashed fleece, it is desirable to cover the knees with a cloth or apron.

Applying oil

After teasing washed fleece, a small quantity of olive oil should be mingled into it before the carding process begins. Avoid corn oil or other vegetable oils as they quickly become sticky and often stain the fibres. Animal fats are not suitable. The olive oil should be used

22 Teasing the fleece

extremely sparingly and preferably sprayed on lightly. The fibre mass should then be folded over to enclose the oil in the centre, then drawn apart between the two hands. Placing the two handfuls together one on top of the other, and again drawing them apart whilst maintaining fibre alignment will spread the oil evenly. Excessive handling in this way should be avoided, as the remainder of the blending will take place during carding.

Unwashed fleece will sometimes also benefit by the application of a little oil. This can be discovered by trial, and also by preference or otherwise. A mixture of one part oil and one part water, plus a half part of ammonia to emulsify the two, is also an economical alternative.

It should be mentioned here that in Britain farmers can sell their clip (i.e. all their fleeces) to the British Wool Marketing Board either 'Greasy' or 'Washed'. These terms have not quite the same meaning as those referred to so far and should not be confused. The hand spinner should procure a 'washed' fleece for choice. This means that the farmer has run his flock through a clear water dip-tank or a stream about three days or more prior to shearing, thus removing excess dirt and grease. The fleece weighs less, but a higher price is commanded as there is less waste. Unfortunately for the hand spinner, this pre-shearing wash is much less common than was wont.

Carding and rolling
Carding

The purpose of the carding process is to align, thoroughly, all the fibres and to spread them

23 *Above* Placing the fleece on the left-hand carder

25 *Below* Starting to transfer the fibres from the left-hand to the right-hand carder

24 *Above* The first carding (N.B. left-hand palm uppermost)
26 *Below* Completing the transfer

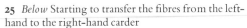

evenly across the carders. This process is essential for the production of a woollen thread and is often employed in preparation for a semi-woollen and semi-worsted yarn.

1 Place the left hand card (this should be permanently marked 'L') on the left knee inclined slightly towards the body. The handle should be grasped with the palm uppermost.

2 With the right hand, apply the prepared fleece firmly and evenly across the card draw-

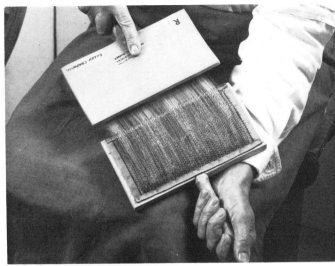

27 *Above* Returning the fibres to the left-hand carder following the second carding (see figure 129)
29 *Below* Completion of transfer of fibres to the left-hand carder

28 *Above* Resuming carding with the right-hand carder (third carding); repeat figures 25 and 28 for the fourth carding
30 *Below* Doffing the fibres to lie on the surface of the right-hand carder prior to rolling

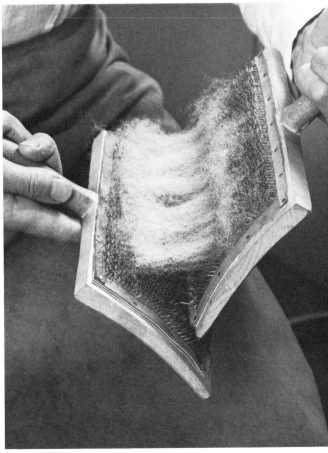

ing against the direction of the wire hooks (figure 23). The correct amount to apply will be found with practice and this will vary depending on the thickness of the yarn required to be spun.

3 Take the other carder (marked with an 'R') in the right hand, palm facing downwards, and with the index finger forward onto the back of the carder itself, draw this carder *lightly* across the left-hand carder repeating the action about six times in a circular lateral movement (figure 24). The fibres will already have begun to align and even out. Any remaining foreign matter, such as particles of hay, may fall out during this process, but it is advantageous to remove any persistent pieces by hand.

4 The next stage is to transfer the remainder of the fibres from the left-hand carder to the right-hand carder. Without changing the position of the hands on the handles, turn the right-hand carder face upwards. Put the bottom edge of the left-hand carder to the handle edge of the right-hand carder. Using a certain amount of pressure, move the two carders in opposite directions, thus enabling the fibres to be transferred firmly onto the right-hand carder (figure 25). It is necessary to keep the two carders at an angle of 60° whilst doing this, otherwise many of the fibre ends will be caught up and doubled back onto themselves. (This causes a ridge of doubled over fibres along the edge of the card which in turn impairs the effective use of the rolag.) If the fibres are protruding beyond the lower edge of the left-hand card prior to the transfer, the wire hooks along that lower edge should engage those on the right-hand carder far enough below its handle edge to allow space for these protruding fibres to lie within the carding area (figures 25 and 26).

5 Carding is then resumed, i.e. the left-hand carder returns to its original position on the lap, and the right-hand carder is drawn across it approximately six times, as before. This action should normally be light. On no account should the carders be forcefully slammed together, and it is important to avoid breaking the fibres by too rigorous an action.

6 After this second carding the fibres should be returned to the left-hand carder. To do this, turn the right-hand carder into a face upward position as before (again remembering not to change the position of the hands on the card handles). Placing the lower edge of this right-hand carder near to the handle edge of the left-hand carder, draw them firmly across each other at an angle of about 60°, so transferring the fibres back onto the left-hand carder (figure 27).

7 Carding is again resumed with the left-hand carder held on the lap as before (figure 28). Remember that the movement of the right-hand carder is a circular lateral one, as described initially.

8 Transfer the film of fibres back to the right-hand carder as described in stage 4. Card again, about six strokes, and transfer from the right-hand carder to the left-hand carder. The transferring from L to R, R to L, L to R, and finally R to L (four changes in all) should be sufficient to produce a perfect rolag. Beware of overcarding as this damages the fibres.

9 The fibres are now ready to be removed. Transfer from the left-hand to the right-hand carder in the manner used previously, but using less pressure, and immediately return it to the left-hand carder. Repeat this using a progressively lighter touch until this film of fibres is lying flat but free on the face of the right-hand carder (figure 30).

Rolling

The aim of rolling is to produce a rolag. Rolags are essential for the production of a true woollen spin, as extensive drafting and a high air content is paramount. Rolags can also be used in the spinning of a semi-woollen yarn. There are two major methods of rolling.

First method
1 Place the left-hand carder face downwards on the knee, with the handle pointing to the left.

2 Shake the fibre film onto the flat wooden back of this carder.

3 Give it a single pat with the back of the right-hand carder.

4 Lay your left-hand palm downwards firmly on the fibre film, and, with the edge of the right-hand carder, lift up an edge of about 1 in (2.5 cm), and press it down so that it is folded back onto itself (like turning up a hem).

5 Lift this 'folded' edge with the carder and roll it across the remainder, travelling it lightly but firmly across from right to left. This should result in a cylindrical roll, which is held in this condition by reason of the outer fibre edge adhering to the main area of the roll. This is known as the *rolag*.

Second method
An alternative and commonly used method of rolling is to do this with both hands on the card clothing side of the card. (Card clothing is the term used to describe the wire hooks set in leather covering the face of each carder.)

1 Place the right-hand carder face upwards on the knee, with the flat loosened fibre film ready to roll, and the handle pointing towards the body.

2 Curl the further fibre edge towards the body with the fingers and thumbs of both hands, and roll it across the card clothing (figure 31).

3 A firmer, closer roll can be produced by placing this rolag at the further edge of the carder and rolling it firmly forwards a second time.

Carding faults

Imperfectly made rolags cause spinning problems. A common fault is the ridge that develops along one edge as carding proceeds. This is due to the doubling over of the fibres during transference from card to card. Or it may be due to catching the protruding fibre ends when proceeding to card again, thereby doubling them back on themselves.

After transference it is often an advantage to flick the *back* of the empty carder across the fibres to firm them onto the hooks of the carder holding them.
Card *lightly*, transfer *firmly* and do not allow fibre ends to project beyond the handle edge of the card. When transferring, engage part way down the carder, holding these more or less at right angles. Start carding at the lower edge of each carder and gradually move across until, by the fourth or fifth stroke, the whole

31 Rolling the rolag

of each carder is in use. Follow the curve of the carders. On average give about six strokes in the carding process and four transferences. Do not overcard. This damages or breaks the fibres. The fibres should be totally aligned and evenly distributed. Roll evenly and firmly. If too loosely rolled, control in spinning is impaired. Short stapled fibres including cotton need a small compact roll for best results.

Quantities to prepare

When preparing rolags in readiness for spinning it is desirable to make a sufficient number to keep one going for an adequate length of time. The constant switching from spinning to carding at frequent intervals leads to a lack of rhythm in the former, and a less satisfying result. Rolags, however, should, if possible, be spun within a day or two of their having been made, as the fibres will flow more freely in the spinning process. Rolags should be placed in a flat basket or box and disturbed as little as possible. Refrain from squashing or pulling them out of shape.

Carded lock method

For semi-worsted spinning, a carded lock is made by rolling the carded fibre film *across* the carder, so that the fibres are in alignment for spinning.

Combing

Wool combing proper, to make a true worsted yarn, is an elaborate process requiring considerable time and skill. The equipment needed and an outline of the method is given in chapter 6. There is a revival of this process today and the necessary tools can be procured from various sources. A simpler form of combing, however, using a dog stripping comb, will be found satisfactory for the majority of spinners aiming to produce a yarn of a true worsted character.

32 Combing a lock with a dog stripping comb (note the combed locks on the left)

During the combing process, a newly sheared fleece will need no addition of olive oil to the fresh natural oil still present. A very light spraying of the locks will suffice if the fleece has become dry or has had to be washed.

Combing with a dog stripping comb

1 First select a suitable type of fleece. Sort it thoroughly. A lustre type is usually ideal. The staple length must be adequate, between say four and twelve inches. The fibre diameter will vary according to the use to which the resultant yarn is to be put (for example a Shetland for a gossamer-like thread, a Devon Longwool for dress or furnishing fabric, etc).

2 Clamp a dog stripping comb to the edge of a table or shelf, or on a spool rack.

3 Carefully select and separate a number of locks of approximately equal size from the area of fleece to be spun.

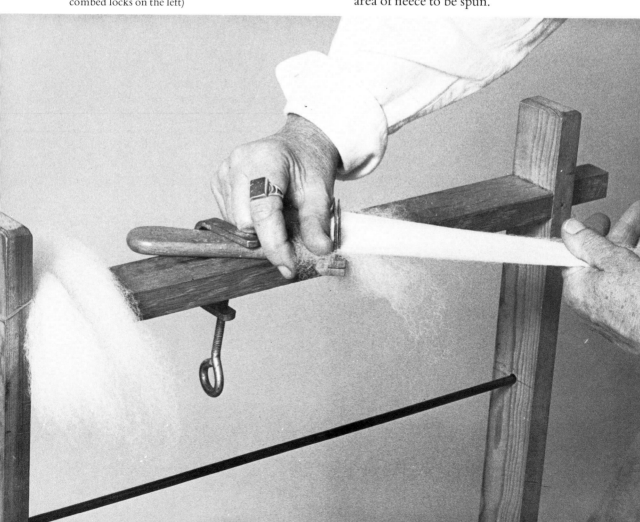

4 Taking one lock and holding it firmly between the finger and thumb with the root end in the hand, place it onto the prongs of the comb about 1 in (2.5 cm) from the tip end of the lock. Draw it gently through, being very careful not to break the fibres (figure 32).

5 Repeat this process, combing deeper into the length of the lock each time until the centre is reached.

6 Reverse the lock in the hand, and repeat this process from the root end of the lock. When the operation is completed the fibres should be perfectly aligned and free, and of uniform length. The shorter fibres retained on the comb should be removed from time to time and set aside for carding for another purpose.

7 The locks should be carefully piled up, with the tips in one direction, and in such a way that they will receive the minimum of disturbance. They are then ready for spinning.
Alternatively the locks can undergo a further stage of being turned into a continuous overlapping sliver known as a 'top'.

Making a top

1 Place a series of locks one upon the other in sequence with an overlap of half the staple length.

2 Carefully draft this length between the two hands, and even it out in the overlapping area.

3 Should this produce too thin a sliver (or top) two or more of these prepared lengths can be laid on top of each other and a final drafting effected between the two hands, the right hand drawing the fibres and the left hand controlling the tension. The two hands should work sufficiently closely together to keep the tension on all the fibres, thereby maintaining the necessary and perfect alignment. This doubling of tops in the drawing also helps to produce an even blend throughout.

4 The resultant length can be coiled on the ground as the drawing proceeds or can be rolled up into loose balls in readiness for use. It is helpful to apply a very small amount of twist in this coiling or balling stage. Incidentally as a worsted yarn is always plied, further evening out can be produced in the plying of two slightly different qualities of singles.

Positioning the equipment

Much waste of time and energy can be eliminated if a little thought is given to the arrangement of materials and tools around one. Teased fleece can be placed at a convenient height and distance on one side while carding, and the rolag basket placed near at hand on the other. Have the wheel within reach, but well clear of the circular movement area needed for carding.

A good light coming from the best angle, and a suitably coloured plain covering over the knees and on the floor is a great help especially when spinning a very fine thread. The height of the stool is also very important, and this will vary according to the individual and the height of the spindle on the spinning wheel which is in use.

5 Spindle spinning

There are many variations within the art of spindle spinning, and many types of spindles (see figure 2). Spindle spinning can be a most enjoyable occupation, and a capable spinner will produce a surprisingly large output. The finest possible yarn can be produced this way, as in cotton spinning and fine silk, on a tiny spindle. Yarn of all sizes (counts) can be produced up to the heaviest, chunkiest imaginable thread. Some of the heaviest of yarn designs can, in fact, only be satisfactorily achieved on the spindle, which in its turn would require to be large, robust and heavy.

Another great advantage of the spindle is that it is comparatively inexpensive. It is also a very mobile piece of equipment as it can be carried about in a capacious pocket or a small bag. Moreover the spinner is able to move around whilst spinning, if desired. Lastly, but not least, the ability to spin on a relatively simple piece of equipment means that many initial difficulties experienced when first using a wheel are already overcome.

The several methods described below are for an average sized spindle, a medium stapled fleece, and a yarn of average count, working from (i) rolags, (ii) combed locks, (iii) direct from the fleece.

As has already been seen, a rolag is made by aligning all the fibres into an even film on the carder and then rolling them to form a cylindrical roll. The process of spinning a *woollen thread* requires the maintenance of the air-filled character of this 'cylinder', by elongating it and applying twist. Therefore the less the rolag is disturbed by handling the better. Sections are drafted and twist gradually introduced as required. The fibres will tend to move in all directions and the resultant yarn will be spongy and air-filled. This is an essential quality of a woollen thread.

All other methods of spinning tend to align the fibres to flow directionally into the yarn, causing a smoother, more solid thread; they are usually worked from combed locks but may also be worked direct from the fleece.

Spinning from a rolag
Woollen spin

1 Attach a 2 ft (60 cm) length of adequately strong wool yarn, not too smooth, to the base of the spindle just above the whorl. This yarn should have a clockwise twist or ply to it, i.e. the diagonal line of the twist on the thread should lie in the direction of the down stroke of a Z. Hitch the yarn over the hook at the head of the spindle, using a half hitch, and allowing at least 8 in (20 cm) of free thread.

2 To join, hold the end of the thread with the finger and thumb of the left hand. Allow the rolag to lie over the back of this hand, and bring the end to overlap the thread about 1 in (2.5 cm). Hold this within the finger and thumb grasp also.

3 Rotate the spindle with the right hand with a sharp clockwise flick, and immediately begin to draw a few fibres from the rolag tip downward along the surface of the thread. The twist in the thread created by the rotating spindle will cause these fibres to attach themselves in a thin film over the yarn's surface.

4 Rotate the spindle again, place the finger and thumb of the right hand onto the centre of this join. Move the left hand very slightly up the rolag, cradling it lightly to avoid damaging it; take a new firm hold and begin to draw upwards.

5 The twist already present above the right hand will run upwards to create the beginnings of a short length of yarn. More twist, however, will be needed to give it strength, so release the grip of the finger and thumb of the right hand, thus allowing twist to run into the whole length of new yarn. This initial length of new yarn will be comparatively short, say 12 in (30 cm) from the join.

6 Rotate the spindle again if more twist is required in the yarn.

7 Maintaining a firm hold on the juncture of yarn and rolag, unhitch the thread from the spindle's hook. Hold the spindle in the right hand at arm's length and in a horizontal position. Begin to wind on by twisting the spindle in a clockwise direction. Build up the yarn package from the spindle base, leaving the top half of the shaft free. Leave a sufficient length to hitch over the hook, and retain about 6 in (15 cm) of yarn above the hitch (figure 58).

8 Rotate the spindle as before. It may be necessary to give it about three separate flicks to achieve sufficient accumulation of twist for the full drafting action for a true woollen spin.

9 Immediately following the last rotating flick, grip the yarn between the finger and thumb of the right hand at a point about *halfway* between the left hand and the spindle head. Release the firm hold of left hand and, cradling the rolag lightly, move this hand up the rolag about 3 in (7 cm), grip firmly again, and draw upwards. The twist will race upwards from the spun yarn that is above the grasp of the right hand. More twist will be needed, therefore release the grip of this hand, and allow further twist to flow upwards from the rotating spindle. If required, draft further between the two hands to produce a finer and more even thread up to 36 in (91 cm) long.

10 Release the grip of the right hand yet again, and rotate the spindle. This will give more twist to the entire length of newly spun yarn.

11 Unhitch the yarn and wind it onto the spindle as described in stage 7.

It is not always possible at first to gauge the degree of twist needed at any one stage in the process. If too much twist is allowed to run into the yarn before it has been sufficiently drafted it will be found impossible to produce a satisfactory thread. This difficulty can be overcome by an untwisting action on the part of the right-hand finger and thumb which grips the thread below the length that is being spun. This is done by moving the forefinger backwards along the length of the thumb, and in so doing, removing the excess twist, and enabling the left hand to draft further. The over-thick length of yarn is thus reduced to its requisite size.

Semi-woollen spin

Bearing in mind that fibres in a rolag lie round and round the roll, one must realise that in any form of drafting these fibres will inevitably be drawn in a number of different directions, and some will even be folded back on themselves. In a short drafting process they will tend to be drawn in the direction of the yarn alignment, but the thread will still retain a degree of variation in this respect and a reasonable proportion of air content.

1 Prepare the spindle as described in stage 1 for woollen spin.

2 Holding the end of the thread and the tip of the rolag so that they are overlapping each other by about 1 in (2.5 cm), rotate the spindle in a clockwise direction, draw down a few fibres with the finger and thumb of the right hand, and allow them to adhere to the twisting thread.

3 Continue a short downward drafting action throughout, keeping a rhythmic rotation of the spindle to produce an even amount of twist in the yarn.

4 When the length spun has reached the maximum that one can operate between the two hands (longer lengths can be controlled when in a standing position rather than when sitting), maintain a firm hold on the juncture of yarn and rolag, remove the half hitch from the spindle head, hold the spindle horizontally at arm's length, and wind onto the base of the spindle above the whorl in a crisscross movement (figure 58). Re-hitch, and continue as before.

5 To join, overlap the new rolag onto the last 1 in (2.5 cm) of the old, so that the two fade into each other. The 'join' will thus be indistinguishable.

6 Repeat from stage 3 onwards.

Spinning from combed locks
Semi-worsted spin

The method is similar to the previous one in that the drafting action is short, and the rhythmic twisting and drawing is maintained in the same way.

1 Take a lock, and overlap it with the end of the starting thread. Twist the spindle and draw down a few fibres. It is necessary to work from a V shape, and the left hand should hold the lock firmly enough to preserve the fibre alignment and allow for a constant number of fibres to be drawn out from it in a V shape with the right hand. To prevent twist from running up into the lock, the top of a middle finger of the left hand can be pressed against the lower point of the V whilst the winding on operation is effected. Spin from the butt end of the lock.

2 Unhitch, wind on, re-hitch and continue the repeated 'twist and draft' process to arm's length before again winding on. Remember that the fibres should be aligned throughout. As plying will probably follow, a fairly high twist is needed in the initial spinning.

Spinning direct from the fleece
Semi-worsted spin

This method will again result in a semi-worsted yarn. That is to say, the fibres will be mainly aligned in the yarn, but will be of varying lengths. The easiest way is to separate the area of fleece to be spun into convenient sized locks. Use a similar process to that described above for combed locks. A more

varied textured yarn will probably result, but this can be attractive and appropriate, and often time-saving if the fleece lends itself to this type of spinning.

Correcting faults

Finding the right weight of spindle for the type and size of yarn is important and will overcome most common problems. A very fine yarn from short stapled fibre source usually requires a small lightweight spindle, possibly supported at its tip when twisted. A thick, high twist yarn will require a large heavy whorl and a long spindle shaft, a medium length staple and a thick firmly made rolag. A relatively small amount of spin on the spindle will produce adequate twist.

Spindle wobble is experienced if the shaft is warped or the whorl not set at right angles to it. It should be spherical and in proportion to the spindle shaft. The yarn should pass over the whorl, round the point of the spindle and subsequently up to the spindle head and hitched over it. The drafting zone should not be less than 6 in (15 cm) from the spindle head.

The most common initial difficulty is the backwards twirling of the spindle before the drafting action is completed. This applies particularly in a long draft woollen spin. Sufficient extra twist must be applied at the outset of each draft, and drafting must be speeded up if necessary. It also happens when spinning a thick yarn, and can be overcome by lengthening the drafting zone (in whatever type of spin) and using a longer distance between spindle top and spinning zone.

Dropping of the Spindle through insertion of insufficient twist is another common fault. Increase the number of twirls on the spindle prior to drafting, or reduce the drafting zone.

6 *Wheel spinning*

The mechanics of the spinning wheel

There are a great many types of spinning wheels. They have been developed along different lines in various parts of the world, and have been designed for a wide variety of purposes. The main categories which have emerged relate principally to the raw fibres to be spun, for example, short fibre wheels (or spindle wheels) have been developed for wool, and other short fibres, and long fibre wheels (the Saxony wheel) for flax, hemp and long wools. Quite different types of wheels have been designed for cotton and silk.

It is the Saxony type wheel (or flyer wheel) which has come to be used as an all-purpose wheel, though there are innumerable variations in styles within this category.

The two types of wheels in general use today are the two-band wheel and the single-band wheel. Most wheels function under the same underlying principles as one or other of these.

Two-band wheel

Often referred to as the Norwegian-type wheel (Norway has been the principal supplier of this kind of wheel in recent years), this type more correctly comes under the general term Saxony wheel (figure 33). It is also known variably as a *flyer wheel* or a *treadle wheel*.

A general purpose and well built wheel of this type has a medium sized *orifice* or aperture (1) in the spindle head, through which the thread is directed onto the bobbin by means of the flyer.

The *spindle* (2) is supported horizontally between two uprights, the front and back *maidens*, (3 and 4) in such a way that it rotates freely without friction. The spindle shaft is of metal, usually iron, or mild steel, having an orifice at the spinning end, and a horseshoe-shaped wooden frame called a *flyer* (5) fixed per-

manently to it, and also a removable *bobbin* (6) held in place on the spindle shaft within the confines of the flyer. There is a two-grooved wooden *whorl* (7) screwed onto the shaft beyond the bobbin. This end of the bobbin also has a groove, which is of smaller circumference than the two on the whorl, and adjacent to it. Along the length of the arms of the flyer are a series of small metal *guide hooks*, which in turn guide the yarn onto the bobbin, enabling an even build up of the yarn as spinning progresses. The framework upon which the maidens, together with the bobbin and flyer, are held is collectively known as the *mother-of-all* (8), which can be adjusted by means of the *adjustment screw* (9).

The *drive* (or driving) *band* (10) is placed in one of the grooves on the spindle whorl (for most purposes the larger whorl groove is used as it gives a greater differential with the bobbin groove and so facilitates winding in of the yarn) and on round the wheel, and then round the spindle and wheel again (thereby crossing itself). The drive band is a cord of relatively high twist and smoothness, just sufficient to avoid either slip or drag on spindle or bobbin. It should be crossed once only (as it runs twice round the wheel and spindle unit) and the ends sewn together or spliced when the mother-of-all is in the central position; this allows for adjustment in either direction.

When the *driving wheel* (11) is in motion (by treadling), the bands drive both spindle and bobbin. The *treadle* (12) attached to the *treadle bar* (13) drives the wheel through the connecting rod, known as the *footman* (14). A *treadle cord* (15) connects the footman to the treadle, and this can be adjusted to alter the working angle of the treadle to suit the spinner. The top of the footman is connected to a curved extension of the wheel's axle, known as the *crank* (16). The wheel itself is suspended on its axle by two *uprights* (17) attached to the *table* (18)

33 The Saxony wheel: (1) orifice, (2) spindle (obscured), (3) front maiden, (4) back maiden, (5) flyer (the guide hooks are obscured), (6) bobbin (obscured), (7) whorl, (8) mother-of-all, (9) adjustment screw, (10) drive band, (11) driving wheel, (12) treadle, (13) treadle bar, (14) footman, (15) treadle cord, (16) wheel bearings for axle and crank (obscured), (17) upright, (18) table, (19) spare bobbins, (20) platform, (21) wheel alignment adjustment bars, (22) tension screw

or stock. *Spare bobbins* (19) are stored between the *platform* (20) and table.

The bobbin groove, being smaller in circumference, causes the bobbin to rotate at a slightly higher speed than the spindle shaft. If a thread is attached to it, looped over a hook on the flyer, threaded through the orifice, and then held in the spinner's hand at tension (this acting as a slight brake), twist will be inserted into the thread. When the tension is released, the thread will be drawn onto the bobbin. If this action is used intermittently, following the drafting and twisting of the fibre supply (rolags or locks) in the hand, the yarn will be spun and fed into the spindle unit in a continuous rhythmic movement.

The *adjustment bars* (21) can be used to swivel the driving wheel slightly for more accurate alignment with the bobbin and flyer groove.

Further control is possible by means of the tension screw (22). This is a wooden screw (occasionally of metal) with which the spinner can move the mother-of-all nearer to, or further away from, the wheel. This variation alters the tension on the bands and changes the rate at which the yarn will wind onto the bobbin. A tight band draws the yarn in rapidly; a slack band draws it in slowly, and creates a lot of twist. Careful and accurate adjustment is all important. A secondary tension adjustment is found by transferring the band onto the smaller diameter spindle whorl.

Single-band wheel and Scotch tensioner (or friction band)

This method of adjustment may have originated in Scotland, as the name suggests, but has undoubtedly also been used with significant variations in other parts of Europe and elsewhere for centuries. The principle of the spinning mechanism is virtually the same as above, but in this type the flyer rotates around the bobbin whilst twist is being inserted and drafting being performed. The bobbin begins to revolve when tension is removed from the thread, and the yarn winds on.

The single band from the wheel drives the spindle, and a short thin band with a stretch device (a strong elastic band or small spring) attached to its end rides over the bobbin whorl (pulley) and is tensioned by turning a small screw or peg to which it is attached. There are many variations on this drag or brake system. The adjustment potential gives perfect control when used in conjunction with the larger tension screw mechanism, which moves the mother-of-all to adjust the drive band.

Classification of spinning techniques

1 *Woollen spin* – spun from a rolag using the long raw technique.

2 *Semi-woollen spin* – spun from a rolag using a short drafting technique.

3 *Semi-worsted spin* – spun from a lock or direct from the fleece, using a short drafting action.

4 *Worsted type spin* – spun on the left-hand side when using a wheel, using combed locks with fibres aligned to the yarn direction and a short drafting action.

5 *True worsted spin* – spun from tops (prepared using woolcomber's tools) on the left of the wheel, the fibres aligned to the yarn direction in a short drafting action, with relatively high twist, and the yarn subsequently plied.

Woollen spin

1 When the wheel has been set ready for use, attach a thread to the bobbin on the spindle, place it around the first hook on the flyer, and thread it through the spindle orifice. Hold the thread protruding from the spindle head in the left hand. Hold the rolag in the right hand. Rotate the wheel. Attach a few fibres from the tip of the rolag along approximately 6 in (15 cm) of thread (figure 34), and 'lose' the end

in the enveloping fibres (figures 35 and 36).

2 Place the finger and thumb of the left hand on the thread, gripping it at a point halfway between the spindle orifice and the rolag juncture, with palm downwards (figure 37).

3 Cradle the rolag lightly in the right hand and slide the hand part of the way up, without damaging the rolag. Take a firm hold in this position (figure 38).

4 Immediately begin to draw out to the right, without releasing the firm hold of the right hand (figure 39).

5 When any section (or sections) along the drafted length (known as the *drafting zone*) needs twist to prevent its further drafting, release the grip on the left hand momentarily only.

6 Draft further (figure 40), still maintaining the original hold by the right hand, and repeat stages 4, 5 and 6 until the yarn is uniform (figure 41) and of the required size (thickness).

7 Introduce further twist to the whole length by removing the left hand, holding the right hand steady and treadling for several more turns of the wheel. This additional twist may not be required. Remember that twist continues to be inserted into the yarn at the winding in stage (i.e. as it moves towards the spindle head).

8 Maintaining the position of the right hand, allow the yarn to be wound into the orifice and onto the bobbin. This means that the right hand holding the yarn moves forwards until it is approximately 9 in (23 cm) from the spindle head.

9 Continue to treadle rhythmically, holding the yarn steady in this position in order to build up a supply of extra twist in this 9 in (23 cm) length (approximately four revolutions of the wheel for averaged sized yarn).

10 Grasp this length of yarn between the finger and thumb of the left hand (palm facing downwards) at a point half-way between the orifice and the right hand. Release hold with right hand, cradle the rolag lightly in this hand, and slide it up about 2 in (5 cm). Take a new firm hold of the rolag at this point.

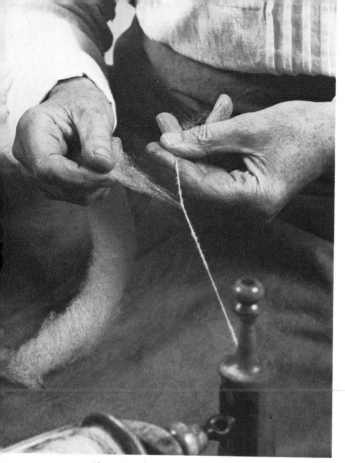
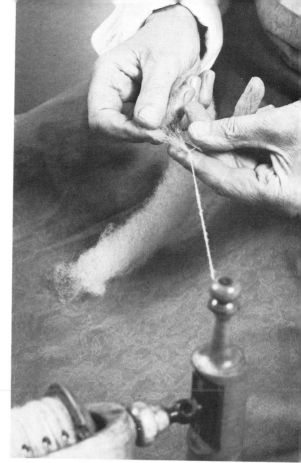

34 *Above* Attaching a few fibres of the rolag onto the thread

35 *Above* Losing the thread in the enveloping fibres
36 *Below* The rolag is now joined to the thread

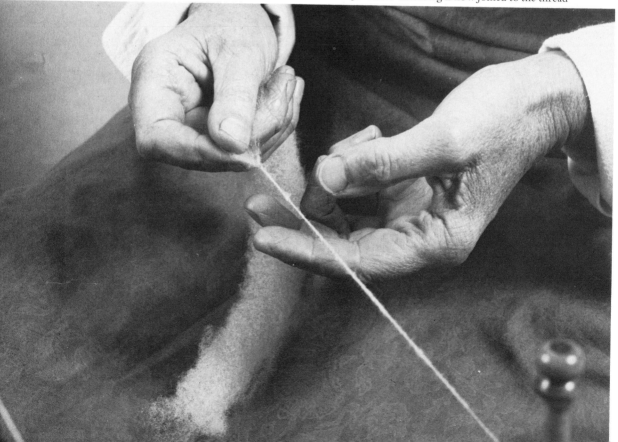

11 Immediately commence to draw out (draft) this section of the rolag. The extra twist will flow into it from the yarn that is to the right of the left hand. When any section is thin enough but requiring twist to give it strength, release the left-hand hold momentarily, and then draft again. (See stages 4, 5 and 6.) Skill and practice are needed to gauge the precise moment to allow twist to run through the left hand, and the amount of twist to apply.

12 Too much twist will prevent the necessary drafting needed and an untwisting action is then required to correct this. It can usually be done whilst the wheel is still in motion. To effect this, untwist the yarn slightly by rolling it backwards across the thumb with the fore-finger. At the same time draft further with the right hand until the yarn is of the required size along its length, and release the left-hand hold. Stages 8 to 11 should be repeated ad infinitum, with the addition, in greater or lesser degrees, of stage 12 where necessary.

13 Very thin places can be corrected only by the addition of extra fibres, either by breaking off the rolag and rejoining as in stage 1, or by

37 *Above* Gripping the joined thread with the left hand
38 *Below* Holding the rolag firmly

39 *Above* Drawing out the rolag
40 *Below* Drafting further to the right

41 *Right* Drafting until the yarn is of uniform size

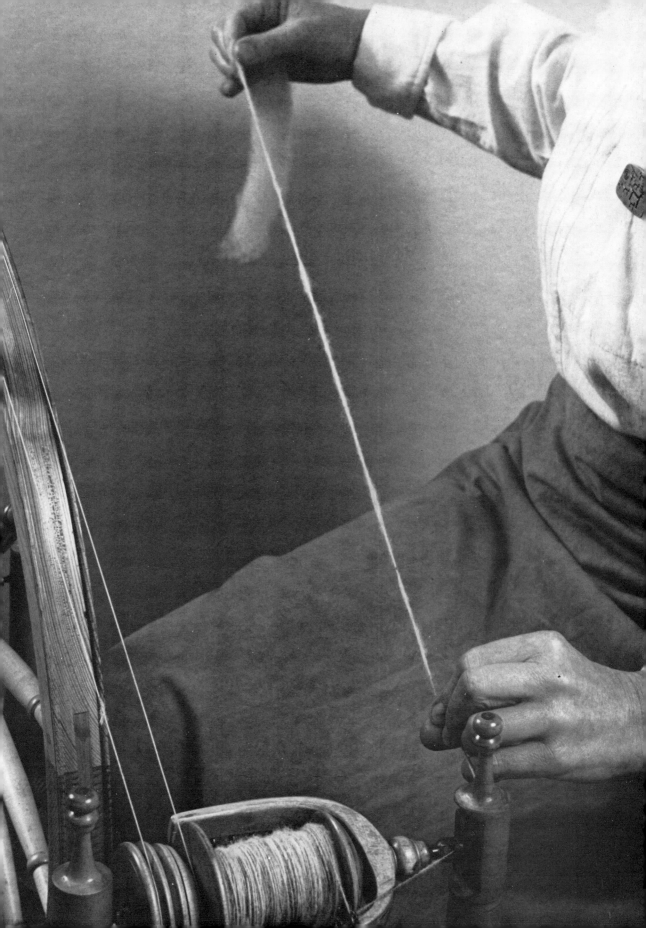

adding a few fibres to the thin area from the other end of the rolag. This needs skill, but it obviates an unwanted join.

The essential feature of the woollen spin is the long draw – i.e. long drafting action. The rolag must be allowed to be elongated and receive twist without any dragging action on the part of the right hand, or mishandling of the rolag. In other words the fixed positions of the hands must be maintained whilst drafting is in progress. The drafting zone is the area between the two hands, and the balance of each consecutive stage will be upset if the right hand is allowed to slide further up the rolag during drafting.

The wheel should revolve continuously in an even rhythm. When one rolag is consumed (it should be spun to the end) another rolag is grafted onto it as described in stages 1, 2 and 3. Note that the drafting begins immediately after the rolag is joined, but in subsequent draftings it is necessary to build up extra spin before moving the right hand into its new position part way up the rolag. Practice will enable the spinner to calculate this.

Should insufficient revolutions of the wheel be given, the twist available will be inadequate and the length of rolag being drawn will disintegrate. A rejoining will be required as for a new rolag.

If too much twist is administered there will be a corkscrew-like overspun thread which will not draft. Stop the wheel gently, and back off with the left hand. Take a new hold on the rolag a little higher up and draft as usual. If the problem is very persistent, suspend the rolag vertically from the orifice and allow the thread above it to unwind. When a normal amount of twist is present proceed in the usual way. As the yarn builds up on the bobbin, move it on to the next hook on the flyer progressively across and back (on average, about every other rolag, but this is arbitrary).

When the bobbin begins to fill it will be found necessary to adjust the tension. The drive band tension must be greater in order to compensate for the diminishing ratio differential between bobbin circumference and whorl circum-ference. By the time the bobbin is reasonably full the drive band should be appreciably tighter than at the beginning. This adjustment is important if a uniform twist is to be maintained throughout.

Semi-woollen spin

A short backward drafting action is used on the rolag for a semi-woollen spin (figure 42). The front hand smooths the fibres as the thread forms, then releases the thread after each draw out, allowing it to be wound onto the bobbin without further handling. By allowing the hands to work quicker in relation to the speed of the treadle, the thread will be given less twist than normal, resulting in a soft, woolly yarn.

Joins are effected by overlapping the new rolag and the end of the previous one and fusing the two in the drafting action.

Worsted type spin
The character of a worsted yarn

The essential character of a worsted yarn is its comparative smoothness and strength. This, however, is relative, as it is largely dependent on the type and quality of the fleece, length of staple, the thickness of the singles yarn, the degree of twist, and the number of twists per inch in the plying. It seems irrelevant to mention commercial yarns in this context, but it is generally appreciated that there are exceptionally fine high twist worsted yarns (Merinos), lustrous medium fine yarns, heavier and immensely strong upholstery worsteds and soft lightly spun knitting yarns worsted spun, to mention only a few contrasting types. Uniform fibre length, alignment in the spin, and a plying process, are common to them all, and should be adhered to in hand spinning also.

There are a number of variations of worsted yarn production known as semi-worsteds, while the true, authentic worsted requires a number of specialised items of equipment for elaborate preparation prior to the spinning

42 Semi-woollen spinning on a Norwegian upright wheel, using a rolag and a short drafting action

process itself (this is described in the true worsted section on page 55).

The following sections describe how to achieve a worsted type spin using (i) combed locks, (ii) a top, and (iii) a folded lock.

Spinning from combed locks

1 Comb a series of separate locks (see chapter 4, page 38). Hold a lock in the left hand with the tip end of the fibres lying towards the spindle head, let the fibres overlap the thread emerging from the orifice, and set the wheel in motion clockwise (figure 43).

2 Grasping a few tip ends of the fibres with the thumb and finger of the right hand draw them forward to enclose the thread, and then immediately slip this finger and thumb backwards, exerting just enough pressure to prevent any twist from running up into the lock. This initial action will produce an adequate join. The drafting zone between the lock and the newly spun thread should be V shaped.

3 As the wheel continues to revolve, draw forward a few fibres with the right hand. Slide this hand backwards about 2 in (5 cm) (again preventing the twist passing through the finger and thumb by creating a little pressure), grip firmly, and draw forward a few fibres. Continue this short backward and forward action rhythmically, paying out the fibres from the left hand as needed. The number of overlapping fibres drawn from the lock must be kept constant in order to maintain a uniform thread. The left-hand hold must be sensitive and just sufficient to aid this.

The V shape must be maintained and it is essential that the twist created by the revolving spindle is not allowed to pass beyond the finger and thumb of the right hand at any time. If this inadvertently occurs whilst spinning a long stapled fleece, the result can be disastrous, as the twist will run into the fibre bundle (the lock) and it will become difficult, or even impossible, to draw out the requisite number of overlapping fibres. A slight downward bending movement when drafting helps to control the twist, preventing it from passing beyond the finger and thumb. Should this

happen, however, it can often be corrected by an untwisting action with the right hand.

4 Before a lock is entirely consumed a new lock should be placed in the left hand overlapping it, and the spinning continued without interruption, except to move the yarn on to another hook on the flyer.

Avoid letting fibres from the lock get out of alignment or allowing them to double back on themselves. Remember that this method is the nearest approach to a true worsted that the majority of spinners attain and should be treated as such.

The yarn spun in this way will normally have much greater twist than that of an average woollen yarn. This is necessary as a worsted spun yarn is plied, and in the process of plying (doubling) part of the initial twist in each of the singles is automatically removed.

Spinning from a top

The method of spinning just described can be followed when using a continuous hand made sliver or top but special care must be taken to avoid letting the fibres move out of alignment or double back on themselves, as this causes a hairy surface to the yarn.

Spinning from a folded lock

Another important alternative method of spinning from the lock is as follows and is almost essential when the fibre length is over 6 in (15 cm).

1 Fold the lock over the forefinger of the left hand.

2 Draw out a few fibres from the fold area along the outer edge of the lock, and attach as usual to the thread that is protruding through the orifice of the wheel by applying twist (i.e. setting the wheel in motion).

3 Continue to draw off from the fold area with the left hand and feed in (figure 47). Move the finger and thumb back each time in an even rhythm. The danger of allowing twist to run backwards into the lock does not apply in this method as the right hand forefinger

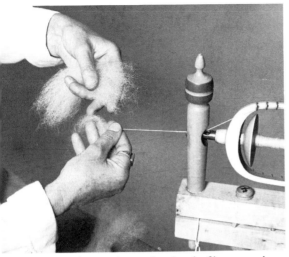

43 Worsted type spin: overlapping the fibres onto the thread

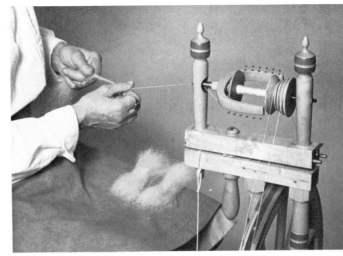

44 Sliding the right hand backwards

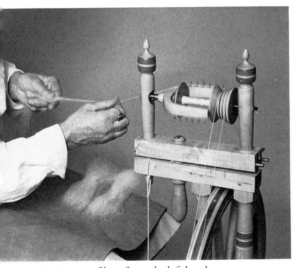

45 Paying out fibres from the left hand

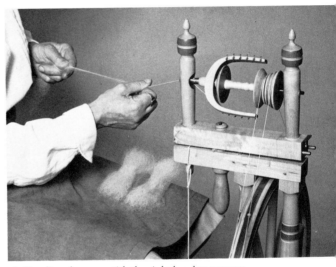

46 Bending the yarn with the right hand to prevent twist from passing back along the lock's fibres

prevents this. (If preferred, the folded lock may be held in the left hand whilst the right hand drafts the fibre flow.)

Semi-worsted spin

This can be spun from carded or combed locks, or direct from the fleece.

1 Splice the lock to the end of the previous one by an overlapping of the film of fibres to effect a join.

2 Maintaining a V shape, draft forward a requisite number of fibres from the V in a relatively short drafting movement and allowing this to wind onto the bobbin in a rhythmic action, holding the lock reasonably firmly (figure 48). Either hand can be used.

3 Alternatively a backward drafting action (i.e. a relatively long draft on the part of the hand holding the lock, followed by a rapid forward winding on) produces a fairly smooth yarn having fibre alignment, and is useful when a light twist is required. It is also speedier with regard to production.

47 *Above* Worsted type spinning from a folded lock

48 *Below* Semi worsted spin, direct from the fleece, using a short forward draft

Correcting spinning faults

Faults in the wheel due to wear and tear or faulty construction need to be rectified by an expert. Wheel adjustments can be made as follows to correct or prevent spinning faults or problems.

Initial difficulty of the winding in of the yarn

Tie the lead thread more tightly round the bobbin core and wind it around several times, clockwise for Z twist and anticlockwise for S twist (this is in reverse if the wheel has a Scotch tensioner).

Overtwisting and not winding in sufficiently fast

Tighten the tension of the driving band (and/or the Scotch tensioner if present). A quarter turn or less of the tension screw is often sufficient. Try also a longer draft and a quicker feed in.

Drawing in too quickly

Slacken the tension on the driving band (and/or Scotch tensioner). The slightest turn is often enough.

Disintegration of the yarn

If the drafted rolag disintegrates or flows apart in the long draw woollen spin, this is either due to (i) an uneven feed in of the twist to the area, (ii) too strong a pull in from the spindle (i.e. too much tension on the drive band), or (iii) possibly a badly made or 'old' rolag. The first must be corrected by allowing just sufficient twist to flow through the left hand whilst drafting (with the right hand) proceeds. In the long draw action this is important. A momentary *untwisting* between the finger and thumb of the left hand is sometimes necessary to facilitate drafting. The hands should not be close together at any time. The right hand must not drag along the rolag prior to drafting, but cradle it gently, and grip it firmly 2 in (5 cm) further up. Too quick a drafting will not give time for the twist to flow up along its length. Too strong a pull-in requires the bands to be slackened (figures 34–41).

In a semi-worsted spin, allow enough twist to pass through the control (left) hand as drafting proceeds. Draft evenly and treadle rhythmically at sufficient speed to create more twist. Open out matted lock tips or whole locks to facilitate more even spinning; spray on olive oil if necessary to assist an even fibre flow.

Snapping of the yarn

If there is too great a build up of twist on a fine yarn this will cause spiralling and a corkscrew effect. Excess twist of this degree may cause the yarn to snap in the thinnest place. Greater tension may be needed on the drive band to allow correct intake of the thread onto the bobbin.

Excess twist is sometimes caused by too fast treadling in relation to the hand movements in the spinning process, thereby causing spiralling. This 'corkscrewed' yarn will be unable to pass freely over the flyer hooks, and the situ-ation is aggravated. Stop treadling, and use up excess twist by moving the right hand well up into the rolag, draft and allow the excess twist to run up into this area, controlled by the left hand. To prevent reoccurrence, try slower treadling and fewer revolutions of the wheel for each drafted length, or a tighter drive band.

Weak joins

Good joins are important, especially in yarn required for warp, as friction from the reed will cause fraying of a weak join. A long draw woollen spin requires an overlap of at least 6 in (15 cm). The fibres from the rolag tip should integrate with the yarn coming from the spindle, *not* spiral round it. Make sure that the last 1 in (2.5 cm) of the yarn becomes enveloped in the new rolag by passing it in with the left hand, placing the finger and thumb of this hand onto the join and drafting a short length from the rolag, then winding in before continuing the usual long draw process. This ensures that the join is wound in, and thus prevents weakening by the long draft action which follows (figures 34–36).

In a semi-worsted spin using carded locks, the new lock must overlap the last 1 in (2.5 cm) of the one preceding it so that integration is total.

The true worsted spin

The object of spinning a true worsted is to produce a very high quality yarn having an absolute minimum of fibre protrusions. The preparatory process needs time, skill, and the use of woolcombers' tools: a pair of wool-combs of a selected size, a diz, a pad, a pan to heat the combs, scales, and a suitable table.

Preparing the fleece

When selecting and preparing a fleece for a true worsted spin it is necessary to sort very carefully into fibre uniformity in both quality and length. Fleece types suitable for worsted belong, in the main, to the Longwool and Lustre group, though very fine worsted yarns are spun from some of the finer, shorter stapled crossbreds, and of course from the Merino.

A short stapled or spongy, highly crimped type is not suitable, nor are the long coarse hair fibre breeds such as the Blackface or Herdwick for example.

The raw fleece should be washed after sorting, keeping the qualities separate. This is important, and must be done with the utmost care. A very dirty or greasy fleece may need several long soakings and several washes and rinses.

When completely dry it is ready for the next stage. This entails drawing out the separate locks from the fleece and laying them out side by side ready to spray with olive oil. A combination of 2 parts olive oil, 1 part water and 1 part ammonia will enable the fibres to comb freely and the moisture will prevent the fibres from becoming unruly due to static electricity created in certain atmospheric conditions during the process of drawing the fibres through the comb. If an aerosol sprayer is not available, an empty plastic squirter (such as that used for liquid detergent) will suffice.

Heating the combs

This is normally required (except in a very warm atmosphere) as the heated combs release the oil content and assist the fibre flow. The simplest and safest method is to immerse the tines (i.e. the teeth of the combs) in a pan of very hot water between each process. The comb head (the base) should never be subjected to direct heat from a hot plate.

Lashing on

One of the combs should be mounted on the pad, and the locks applied one at a time at their butt (root) end building up across the comb, layer upon layer, using only the longest (nearest) row of tines. As it is important to produce tops which are consistently even throughout the preparation, it is advisable to load the comb with the same quantity of fleece each time. If the locks are uniform in size and an equal number applied at each loading, this may suffice, but weighing on sensitive scales is preferable for greater accuracy, say $1-1\frac{1}{2}$ oz

(30–40 g) according to the size of comb. If mixtures of dyed fleece are to be used to produce a coloured roving, exact proportions of each are essential.

Jigging

The next process, known as jigging, is in fact the combing process. Place the comb on its side in the pad. Taking the second comb in the right hand, tines pointing downwards, swing it to catch the *tips* of the locks on the pad comb on the downward stroke. (This is a short curved movement of the hand comb, not an extensive swing.) Repeat this a number of times, gradually moving the hand comb nearer to the tines of the pad comb. Most of the fibres will eventually have been transferred to the hand comb (figure 49). These must then be returned to the pad comb.

To do this the hand comb must be moved in a horizontal anticlockwise circular motion passing the pad comb in such a way that the fibres catch onto its tines a few at a time, until most of them are back on this comb. The vertical combing process and the horizontal transfer are repeated until the fibres are totally evened out, the last combing ceasing when equal quantities are present on each comb.

Then follows the first drawing off into a sliver. Turn the comb into an upright position (so that the tines face upwards'). Stroke the fibres protruding from the comb on the pad into a point, and draw out about 2 in (5 cm). Place the finger and thumb of the other hand about 2 in (5 cm) above the fibres grasping them into a narrow point each time, and draw another 1 in (2.5 cm) of sliver from the mass. Continue drafting with an overhand movement until a length approximately 3 ft (1 m) is achieved. Break this off and lay it on the table. Repeat this process until the comb is empty. The hands should hold the points of fibre mass firmly, and should be placed horizontally and vertically alternately, thus maintaining a more even flow. (For example, grip with the right hand from the side and the left hand from above.)

49 Jigging, gradually transferring the fibres from the pad comb to the hand comb

50 Planking, woolcomber's combs and horn diz (threaded onto the sliver in the centre); the right-hand comb shows the initial stages (i.e. lashing on)

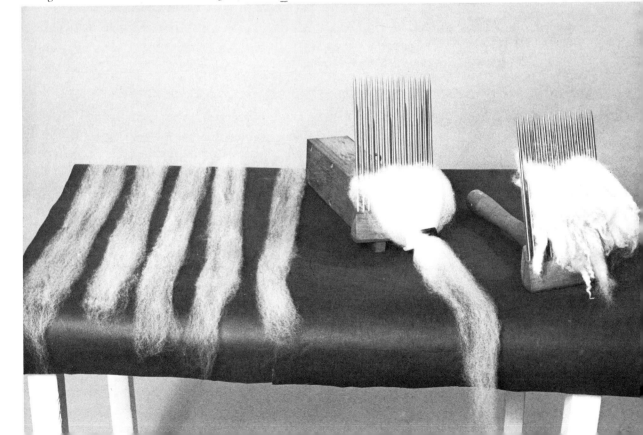

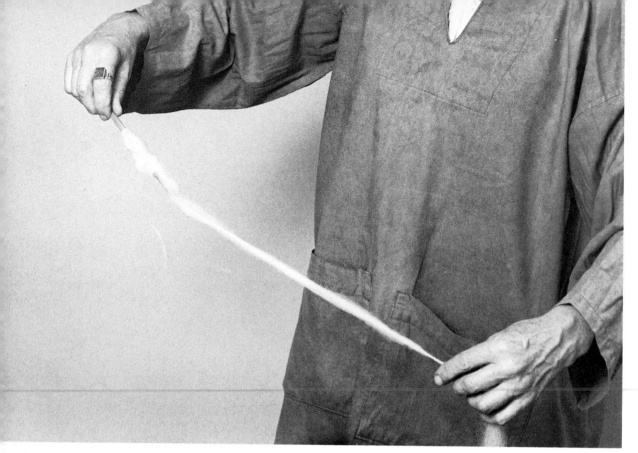

51 Making a top from a planked sliver

Planking

Lay the slivers side by side in the same direction; this is known as planking. Remove the short fibres or noils from the combs. Now begin to apply the tips of the bundle of planked slivers onto the comb, employing all the rows of tines this time. Load the comb by allowing the sliver to break off each time when the protruding piece is about 10 in (25 cm) long. When fully loaded, stroke the ends into a point, thread through the diz (with the curved edge towards the comb), and draw off into a sliver through the extra control afforded by the diz (figure 50). This is a thin ring, usually made of horn, which controls the fibre flow. It needs regular pressing forward towards the tines as drafting proceeds. The sliver or top should be drawn out evenly and allowed to lie untouched, continuing until the whole is used from the comb (avoid the rougher parts at the extreme end – these should be added to the noils for subsequent woollen spinning).

Forming the roving

Lastly a lightly twisted roving is formed by feeding the sliver onto a long-shafted hand spindle, by applying a *very slight* amount of twist and then winding onto the shaft (figure 51). It is necessary to use a supported spindle or a grasped spindle as the sliver would not take the weight of a drop (suspended) spindle. This is a quick process, and even speedier on a long-spindled Great wheel. Whatever method is used the amount of twist must be very slight and even throughout. Spinning can then proceed direct from the shaft or from a ball wound from the shaft.

Method of spinning

As with all types of spinning the amount of twist is of paramount importance in determining the character of the yarn. The softest fleece can have a harsh handle in the yarn if too much twist is applied. Conversely a limp and unsuitable thread can be created by applying too little twist. Total control is easy to attain when the fleece is perfectly prepared as in the woolcombing process described above, and when the wheel is correctly tuned to draw in at the required speed. The drafting action must be precise and constant, but it is necessary to adjust the length of draft between the two hands, related to the revolutions of the wheel, until the required amount of twist is arrived at, and then maintained throughout. A small wheel diameter is an advantage.

1 Take the end of the roving in the left hand, hold the end of the starting thread (opened out) in the right hand, and begin to treadle, splicing the two butts and drafting slightly to effect a join.

2 Keep the finger and thumb of the right hand at the point where the roving 'V's out from the yarn, move the left hand up the roving the desired amount, about 1 in (2.5 cm), and grasp reasonably firmly (figure 52).

3 Move the right hand up towards it, maintaining sufficient pressure to prevent any twist from passing through this hand and into the drafting zone, which lies between the two hands. No twist must ever be allowed to escape into the drafting zone.

4 Draft in a forward action with the right hand (allowing a slight relaxation of the pressure of the left hand on the fibre mass) and immediately move the right hand backwards along the drafted fibres. The twist will follow behind and a 2 in (5 cm) length of smooth yarn will be made. The left hand moves back along the roving as before. The right hand pinches firmly at the point of hold, and drafts again, and once more immediately moves backwards along the drafted fibres.

5 This process (from stage 2 to 4) is repeated ad infinitum keeping exactly the same rhythmic movement and number of fibres drafted, and also the same drafting length and number of twists per inch along this length.

Quality control

Remembering that a quality yarn is the essential criterion, it naturally follows that the spinning process itself requires both skill and

52 True worsted spinning from a top

the utmost care. A knowledge of the spindle-pulley-diameter to wheel-diameter ratio is a great advantage, as the number of twists per inch (TPI) can be a known factor in one wheel revolution (i.e. one treadle action). The speed of wind-on is also a factor which determines the overall twist in the yarn, as does the thickness of the bobbin core when empty. Both this and the size of the spindle pulley groove may need to be altered (the bobbin increased and the pulley decreased) if over-spinning cannot be overcome by lengthening the drafting zone sufficiently without detriment to quality and control.

(The preparation and art of worsted spinning is most excellently and fully described in Peter Teal's book *Hand Woolcombing and Spinning*.)

7 *Plying and direction of twist*

Plying means the twisting of two or more threads together. This twist is usually inserted in the opposite direction to that used in the component singles, i.e. clockwise-spun (Z twist) yarns are plied anticlockwise and vice versa. Variations are infinite and many fancy or effect yarns are plied. *Doubling* normally refers to the plying of two like threads in an opposite twist.

Note that yarn which has been plied should normally be washed, even though the singles may have been spun from scoured fleece. Singles yarn intended for plying should not normally be washed in the skein. A light washing process and a slight stretching of the skein will set and unite it (see chapter 9, page 80).

Plying with a spinning wheel

1 Take two filled bobbins of hand spun singles yarns previously removed from the wheel and put these onto a spool rack or Lazy Kate placed to the right-hand side and beyond the wheel.

2 Tie the hand spun threads from these to the third and empty bobbin on the wheel, to travel through the orifice. If required, a tensioning device can be used to ensure that the yarns run uniformly from each bobbin (figure 53). This also prevents the snarling of high twist yarns behind the right hand.

3 Hold the two threads in the right hand (palm facing to the right and downwards) and the forefinger, or the second finger if preferred, inbetween the two threads. Hold these threads straight and at arm's length.

4 Commence treadling, turning the wheel in an anticlockwise direction (S ply). If the singles yarn has been spun in an anticlockwise direction (S spun), then the plying should be done in a clockwise direction (Z ply).

5 The plied yarn should be fed in regularly and rhythmically, keeping the doubled thread straight – when the right hand is within approximately 6 in (15 cm) of the orifice, slide this hand backwards to arm's length, hold to insert twist into the new length, and again feed in.

The character, strength and bulkiness or fineness of the thread is dependent on the amount of initial twist in the singles in relation to the twists per inch in the doubling process. For example, two fine quality, relatively high twist singles that are plied at a low number of twists per inch will retain most of the initial twist, yet show a clear though comparatively loose ply. Similar singles which are doubled at a relatively large number of twists per inch will lose more initial twist in each thread and become a bulkier rounder thread in the ply.

There are many variations on these two examples, dependent on the type of spin used and character of the fleece employed. After trying out a few yards (metres) it is as well to withdraw it from the wheel and inspect the result before proceeding further.

Plying three or more yarns

Use the same technique as described above, but put a finger between each thread throughout the process, being careful to allow an even tension on each. It should be noted that yarns composed of more than two singles tend to lose character, becoming rounder and less lively. There may be exceptions, however, when colour, fibre and textural variations are apparent in each of the singles. Interesting effect yarns can obtain from such a composition, especially if one of the three has a reverse twist to the other two.

A three ply yarn can also be created from a singles yarn. This is done by chaining between

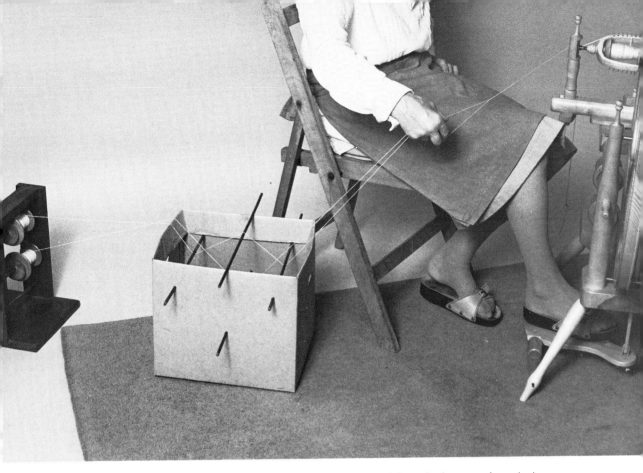

53 The singles yarns from two filled bobbins placed in a Lazy Kate are threaded through a home-made tensioning device before being plied on the spinning wheel

the finger and thumb of one hand, making approximately 8 cm (3 in) long loops, and allowing it to wind forward through the orifice rhythmically. (This stems from the method used by the Navajo weavers.)

Cabling

Cabling is the term used to describe the combining of two plied yarns into a second doubling process, and is not greatly used with hand spun yarns.

Plying from balls of yarn

There are occasions when the spinner might wish to wind the yarn from the bobbin or spindle directly into a ball. It is possible to ply from two or more balls, but it should be noted that it is not possible to maintain an accurate control on the twist and ply ratio. This is due to the fact that the ball will run around (as it

reduces in size during plying), and twist is intermittently and indeterminately removed as it does so. Some control to reduce this can be achieved by placing the balls in small polythene or paper bags, and putting these in a box or basket. The threads pass through a small space in the top of the bag, which is tied with string. As the ball reduces in size, the tie should be moved further down to restrict excess movement of the ball. Make sure that the yarns have an equally free flow from their respective containers, attach them to the bobbin on the spinning wheel, and ply as already described.

Plying without a wheel

Loose twisting together can be effectively achieved with simple apparatus without a wheel. Mount two bobbins one above the other, placed vertically, with at least 6 in

61

(15 cm) between each. A cardboard box, up-ended, suffices, having a hole made in the centre top. Take the yarn from the lower bobbin through the centre core of the upper bobbin. Draw off the yarns from each bobbin together into a ball or onto a spool. The two yarns will automatically spiral lightly round each other at approximately one twist per inch.

Plying with a drop spindle

For those who use a hand (suspended) spindle for the production of a singles yarn, it is logical to use the same tool for the purpose of plying. This is not difficult, but a degree of rhythmic control must be adhered to in order to give the relative or precise uniformity required for most yarns.

1 Prepare two balls of similar size by winding these from the spindle.

2 Place each in a small polythene or paper bag tied at the top to allow the threads to slip easily through the neck. Put these bags in a box or basket and place it on the floor near to the left foot. Alternatively wind the singles yarn onto spools, and run them out from a spool rack or Lazy Kate. It is possible to ply yarns from a ball and a spool at the same time.

3 Tie the two hand spun ends onto the base of the spindle shaft and hitch them to the tip of the spindle.

4 Hold the two threads so that they run on either side of the middle finger of the left hand about 12 in (30 cm) above the spindle head (figure 54).

5 Rotate the spindle in an anticlockwise direction (S ply) if the singles were clockwise spun (Z spun).

6 Slide the left hand up another 12 in (30 cm) approximately. When sufficient twist is present in this length, unhitch the yarn and wind it onto the base of the spindle. Endeavour to keep the singles yarns in position on each side

54 Plying on a spindle using white yarn from a bobbin placed in a spool rack, and natural black yarn from a ball placed in a basket

of the middle finger throughout, and never bring the hand less than 12 in (30 cm) from the spindle head.

7 Gauge the length most convenient for plying and maintain this throughout. Rotate the spindle evenly and give each length the same number of twists per inch. The spindle will become fully laden before the balls are used up. Wind off into a measured skein, preferably using a niddy noddy (see chapter 9). Tie on again, and repeat the plying of the remainder of the balls.

S and Z twist yarns

This applies to all types of yarn and refers to the direction of twist imposed upon the overlapping fibres in spinning. A Z twist is a clockwise twist, i.e. the spindle or wheel is rotated in a clockwise direction. The downward stroke of the Z shows the direction of twist on the yarn. Conversely an S twist is an anticlockwise twist, the down stroke of the S conveying the line of twist in the yarn.

When yarns are plied, as in worsteds, knitting yarns and many other types, two or more Z twist singles would normally be S plied, and vice versa. Special effect and character yarns can be produced by S plying one S and one Z singles yarn, or Z plying one Z and one S singles. In each case one yarn will accumulate more twist whilst the other will lose some of its original twist and become bulkier.

If, when plying, the tension on the yarn receiving more twist is greater, the yarn losing twist will tend to spiral around the finer thread. If the reverse is imposed, the finer, higher twist thread will spiral around the softer bulky yarn. The resultant two plied yarns will be very different. The *angle* of the down stroke of the Z or S in the yarn will vary according to the degree of twist. This is measured in twists per inch (TPI), and contributes to the strength and texture of the end product, whether it is knitted, woven, or crocheted from the yarn. Fabrics must be designed with direction(s) and degree of twist in mind.

8 *Colour and special effects*

55 This woven skirt with a border inlay shows an effective use of yarn hand spun from different coloured fleeces

Coloured yarns
Natural and dyed fleeces

Coloured fleece normally means a non-white fleece, namely a black, grey or brown fleece. A fleece can, however, be dyed before spinning, so the term will here be used to cover both natural and applied colour.

Natural coloured fleeces are rarely completely uniform throughout the whole area, moreover the staple itself usually varies a considerable amount in colour along its length, the tip end (being exposed to the elements of sun and weathering) usually being paler than the root end. Conversely a grey or brown yearling (hog) may have dark points to the tips and a much lighter root end. Whichever is the case the resultant yarn will have a very different appearance from the bundle of undisturbed staple fibres. The mixture may, and probably will, give a lively and interesting effect when spun, but if streakiness is to be avoided the fibres need to be as uniformly blended as possible in carding or combing. The wool of the rarer breeds, such as Soay and St Kilda, should be prepared and spun in such a way as to preserve the beauty of colour variation to the full.

Controlling colour through carding

Most attractive mixtures and blends can be obtained in the use of two different natural coloured fleeces or a coloured and a white. If these fleeces are carefully sorted and carded with equal proportions of each (spread evenly across the carder) the yarn produced will be a true combination of the two. The same will apply to a dyed fleece and a white fleece, or two or more different coloured dyed fleeces. The results are akin to the mixing of paints.

Less fusion of the two or more colours will result in a livelier and more varied yarn, colourwise. It is necessary to experiment with the carding/spinning combination until a satisfactory yarn mixture is achieved; a record should be kept of the proportions, the placing of the fibres on the carder, and the method of carding used in each experiment.

A more intermittent colour variation on the yarn can be achieved in the following way and is essential if short stretches of unbroken single colour or white are to be retained.

1 Place a tuft of white fleece in the centre of the carder and one on each outer edge.

2 In the two remaining spaces, place equal amounts of natural black.

3 Card as usual, transferring from one to another carefully to keep the colours in position and noting how an area of grey emerges between each section.

4 Make a second collection of rolags of the same size, but applying the fibres to the carders in the reverse arrangement.

5 When spinning, take the rolags from each pile alternately. Experiment to test the length of each colour section when spun. This will, of course, be controlled by the relation between the degree of drafting and the quantity of fibres of each colour in the rolag.

Colour effects

If the yarn is used as weft, the visual effect on the woven fabric will vary tremendously according to the width of the warp. For example, if each colour section along the length is approximately 15 in (38 cm) and the width of the warp is 36 in (90 cm), the colour sequence will change constantly on every weft pick. If on the other hand, the warp is, say 8 in (20 cm) wide, the one colour will develop a thicker, striped effect across the fabric. If the warp is similarly variegated, the tendency will be to a variable check-like pattern.

If knitting or crocheting is the intention, then the yarn may need to be plied. In this instance greater difficulty is experienced in finding an overall uniformity, as areas of one colour on each singles yarn may from time to time coincide and at other times be in juxtaposition.

Not much can be done to correct this other than a slight easing up of one of the two singles in the plying process. If, however, an intermittent colour mixture singles yarn is plied with a one colour yarn, the doubled yarn will take on an entirely different appearance, and is worth some experimentation.

Extra bulky yarns

Medium thick yarns can be spun on a flyer wheel (treadle wheel) provided that the orifice is reasonably large. Extra thick yarns need either an outstandingly large orifice, hooks and bobbins to receive them, or the absence of these as found with the spindle or the spindle wheel (i.e. Great wheel). The type of flyers that have these requirements are the Indian Spinner and the Jumbo Flyer, and there are ever increasing varieties of wheels being made to accommodate the special requirements of the modern hand spinner.

If using a spindle, a large size (sometimes extra large) is needed, and this should have a long shaft and an adequately heavy whorl. In the majority of cases it is easier to control the spin of a bulky thread if the fibres are first carded into rolags. These should be thick and fairly dense. If a semi-worsted type yarn is required the fibres can be carded and rolled sideways across the carders, and drawn during spinning from the tip of these carded locks. Long or medium-long stapled fleece will present greater difficulties when drafting a very thick thread, so it is better to choose a fairly short or medium stapled fleece.

Producing bulky yarns using a spindle

Impart a relatively small degree of spin on the spindle and draft rapidly, maintaining a large number of overlapping fibres throughout. If a soft spongy air-filled texture is desired, the spindle should be rotated very little. A bulky thread will hold together with a minimum of twist. A very few more rotations will give it a high twist and greater strength reducing the diameter. If the intention is to make an exceptionally thick thread by subsequent plying, it is

56 *Left* 'Lee Moor II' (from the Dartmoor Winter Series' by Bobbie Cox, 64 × 35 in (162 × 88cm), acquired by the Dartington Hall Trust. The coloured yarns, hand spun from natural black, grey and white fleeces together with dyed fleeces in fawns, ochres and reds, are an essential ingredient in the design of this wall hanging.

57 *Above* Detail of 'Lee Moor II'

58 *Left* Spindle spinning a thick, bulky yarn from a large, two-colour rolag: the winding on process

59 *Above* Producing a thick yarn on an Indian Spinner

necessary to insert sufficient twist in the singles in the first place to ensure that it is not all removed at the plying stage!

Spinning from a rolag using the long draw action of the woollen spin is, on the whole, the easiest and most satisfactory. The result is a lighter weight yarn for its bulk, holding great air content. It is also easier to apply greater twist and therefore more strength. This type will also ply well.

Producing bulky yarns on a Great wheel

The same observations relating to the use of the spindle should be applied to the use of the Great wheel. In the case of especially bulky yarns a very long heavy gauge spindle should be used. The extra 'solid' rolag is drafted slightly, then more twist is added by one turn of the wheel, followed by drafting between

the two hands using a long draw woollen spin, and finally backed off and wound onto the base of the spindle. This base should have a stout piece of brown paper round it onto which the yarn is wound, the whole package being later removed intact. It can then be placed onto a spool rack for winding off onto stick shuttles or for use in plying of heavy rug yarns. (Full instructions on the use of the Great wheel are given on pages 142–148). Some bulky singles yarns are even suitable for knitting on large needles.

Producing bulky yarns using an Indian Spinner or a Jumbo Flyer

It is essential to treadle very slowly indeed, and feed in relatively fast, otherwise the yarn will corkscrew and refuse to pass over the hooks on the flyer. Whichever tool is used it is not possible to produce an entirely uniform thread

69

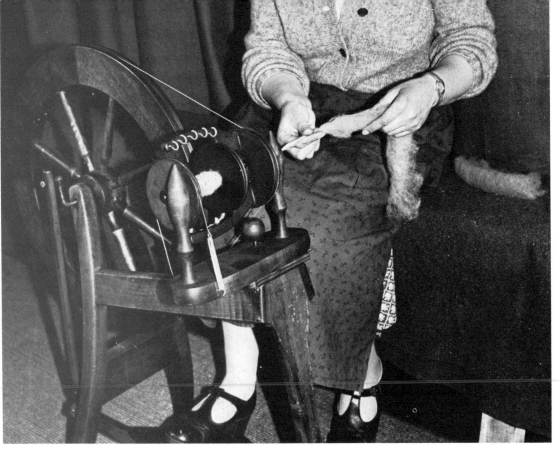

60 Spinning an extra thick yarn from a rolag for floor rugs on a Jumbo flyer attached to an Ashford wheel

61 While the right hand controls the twist, the left hand drafts out the yarn

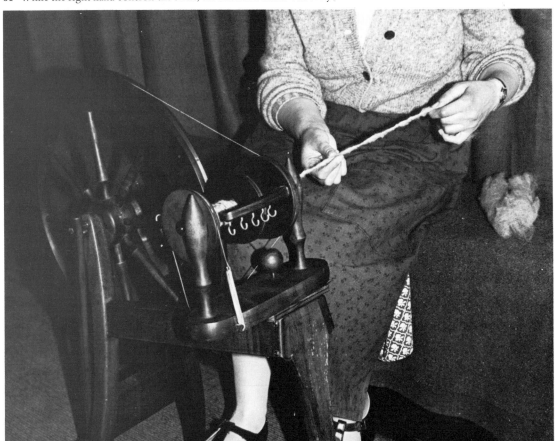

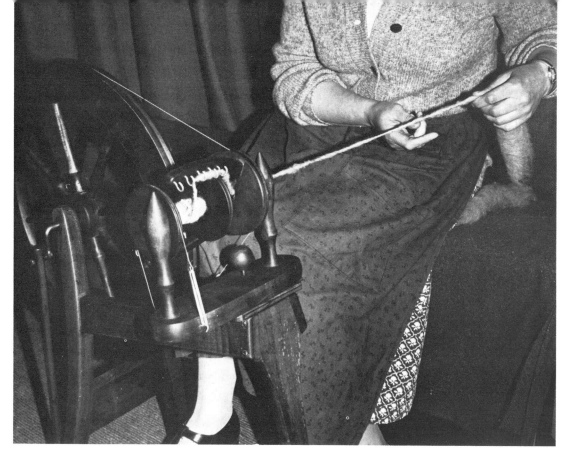

62 Slow treadling, and a fast feed in, produce a relatively consistent yarn

and indeed in this context a perfect uniformity would be undesirable. It is, however, important to maintain an overall regularity to ensure that the character and average size of yarn is kept constant. Yarns of these sizes are often enhanced by the inclusion of colour blends.

Producing bulky yarns by hand

There is a further method of producing a very bulky and spongy charactered yarn and one which is highly suitable for floor rugs. No wheel or spindle is needed. Rolags are carded to hold a large fibre content. A light twist is inserted into the rolag by hand immediately after laying it in the open shed of the warp. This gives it greater strength and a slightly smoother texture. If tonal blending or colour blending is required, two rolags of varying shades can be lightly twisted when inserted across as weft. This method is particularly suitable in the creation of thick, soft-textured floor rugs.

Extra fine yarns

The beauty, excellence and durability of the fine worsteds, fine hosiery, gossamer shawls (figure 64) and much else of the centuries preceding the Industrial Revolution bear witness to the superb skill of the average spinner of those earlier days. There is a place for this quality of craftsmanship amongst hand spinners today. Fleeces are to be found which lend themselves ideally to the creation of the finest and most beautiful of yarns. It is necessary to select a top grade fleece having a fibre diameter graded between 65s and 100s. It must be appreciated that the method of spinning chosen will have a direct and vital bearing on the resultant fineness of the yarn. The character of the fleece will play an equally important role, as will the number of overlapping fibres along the length of the yarn.

Worsted type spin for superfine fleece

This method is commonly used by spinners in the Shetland and Orkney Isles. A fine quality Shetland, of staple length approximately 3 in

71

63 Mounted samples of extra thick and extra fine yarns (from left to right): extra thick 2 ply, thick spindle spun, noils spun yarn, soft spun grey mixture, fine woollen spun (Southdown), fine worsted type spun (Shetland)

64 *Right* A knitted shawl of gossamer-fine 2 ply hand spun wool, approximately 70 years old

(7 cm) for example, can be combed in the lock and spun with ease using a worsted type drafting and just enough twist to establish a gossamer-fine singles yarn of surprising strength.

Draw locks from the sorted fleece as required. Use a fine-toothed dog comb or bone type hair comb in the hand to comb each lock, first working from the tip end to the centre, then reversing the lock and gradually combing the root end to the centre. When a number of these locks have been prepared, place a *small* upright wheel (e.g. a Shetland wheel) in front or slightly to the right of you as you sit. After attaching the first fibres of the lock to the thread protruding through the orifice, by an overlapping and twisting action set the wheel in a gentle, even rotation and proceed to draft a short length between the left hand, which

holds the lock, and the right hand.

This initial draft produces a length of fine yarn approximately 3 in (7 cm). Then take out some of the twist with the forefingers and thumb of the right hand, and draft those 3 in (7 cm) further to produce an extra $1-1\frac{1}{2}$ in (2–3 cm) from it. The left hand has so far held the lock firmly and prevented twist from running up beyond this point. The short length of superfine yarn then winds in towards the bobbin, the left hand moves slightly up the lock, and drafting is repeated between the two hands, plus the second draft to create an extra fine yarn. The rhythm is continuous throughout.

Woollen and semi-woollen spin for an extra fine fleece

The following method is employed when a fine Shortwool or Down type fleece is to be

spun. It requires to be a very fine diameter fibre and a uniform quality, for example the neck and shoulders of a 60s quality or finer Southdown, and must be as matter-free as possible. The fleece should be carefully and thoroughly teased.

A fine diameter Southdown, with staple length approximately $1\frac{1}{2}$ in (3 cm), having many crimps per inch, would first of all need to be carded. It would spin exceptionally well as a fine woollen singles, the weight per given length being similar to the Shetland. The air content and bouncy character would make it appear slightly thicker. A semi-woollen (short draw) method using the rolag would result in a denser yarn of equal fineness but more weight, and also a springier character than that of the Shetland.

Rolags should hold a relatively small number of fibres, and be small and rather tightly rolled and uniform in size. They should preferably be of unscoured fleece, but should the fibres be held together on the surface by an accumulation of dirt and weathering, the fleece may be soaked in warm water and left for a few hours, gently rinsed and then spread on a net to dry. Spinning follows, using either a long draw (woollen spin) or a short draw.

The long draw method
If using the long draw method, remember that the fibres are very short. The large degree of crimp helps to give cohesion, so that drafting using the long draw technique is comparatively easy. A very even rhythmic motion is essential, together with precise control in the left hand. The exact amount of twist and drafting must be established by unwinding the first trial yard (metre) or two and examining it critically. An impressive degree of fineness can be achieved, but care must be taken to avoid masking the resilient character and natural beauty of the fibre.

The short draw method
The short draw method (termed semi-woollen) using a similar small, dense rolag is achieved as follows. Cradle the rolag in the right hand and, holding it near the join between the finger and thumb of the left hand, draft short even lengths between the two hands, allowing a winding on between each draft. Take care to avoid overspinning. This can be corrected by treadling more slowly in relation to the hand movement and/or tightening the bands. The drafting can be considerable to produce a very fine yarn, i.e. one having a similar number of overlapping fibres to that found in the fine woollen spun thread, but denser and therefore apparently finer.

The folded lock method
A further method of spinning an extra fine thread can be employed when the fibre length of a fleece is great, or comparatively so. Lustres, and incidentally some hair fibres, lend themselves to this process, though it is also often used in the production of thicker yarns.

A comparatively fine Longwool Lustre, with a staple length approximately 6–8 in (15–20 cm) could be combed in the lock and given a worsted type spin in which not more than 2 or 3 fibres were incorporated at any one time. This type of yarn has limited usage, but an amazingly strong and fairly fine yarn can be produced by incorporating slightly more fibres, introducing more twist, and subsequently doubling this yarn.

The locks are combed with a dog stripping or other type of comb. Each lock is folded in half over the forefinger of the right hand (figure 47). The left hand drafts, using a forward movement, and the fibres slide into a continuous worsted type yarn, with an intermittent draft and feed-in motion. As one lock is consumed, another is folded over the finger and grafted onto the receding end of the newly spun yarn to overlap about 1–2 in (2–3 cm) before twist reaches the extremity. Yarns of this type are more commonly plied, but if a singles yarn is intended, slightly less twist would be required than normal. Tighten the bands a little and lengthen the draft slightly.

Effect yarns
Yarns which come into the category of effect

yarns, fancy yarns or textured yarns are many and widely varied. They can at once be exciting, delightful and easy to create, or equally beautiful but slow and difficult to produce. They can be extremely fine, extraordinarily thick, beautiful or plain ugly. The hand spinner should use some restraint in the use of effect yarns in an end product. They have a place in some instances but the beauty of high quality yarns of a straightforward simplicity cannot be overrated. The following sections should give rise to individual inventiveness, and some enhancement of textural quality to the resultant cloth if these yarns are used with aesthetic comprehension and restraint.

A combination of wool and a second fibre such as silk, cotton or one of the hair fibres can be used in many of the effect yarns described here. It must be emphasised, however, that not only must the yarn be soundly constructed, but also the fibre behaviour in subsequent processes and ultimate usage must be fully anticipated and understood in the context of the designing of the yarn. The following points should be borne in mind:

1 Bulky, lightly twisted yarns or parts thereof (as in slubs) will have a tendency to felting, especially if the fleece is a Longwool.

2 A high twist yarn can cause a harsh handle and sometimes a crepe-like character to a woven fabric when this effect is not intended. It is not usually suitable for knitting, and dye penetration is also impeded.

Slub yarns

Variations on a slub yarn include thick, thin, long, short, intermittent, one colour, two or more colours, singles, plied, and one slub plied with one fine singles, as in a spiral slub, etc. The basic method is as follows. Using a rolag and a semi-woollen short draft, take a small number of fibres between the finger and thumb of the left hand, and draft forward to

65 Mounted samples of effect yarns (from left to right): silk and alpaca mixture rolag, silk and alpaca mixture yarn, slub yarn, four rolags showing alternate black and white sections, white random spiralled 2 ply yarn, yarn spun direct from the fleece using black and white locks concurrently, spiral-wrapped two-colour yarn

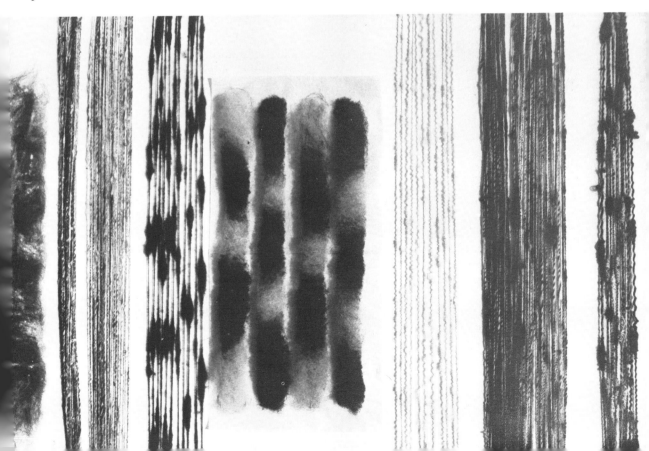

produce a relatively fine yarn. Follow this with a large number of fibres in a forward draft movement and a minimum number of wheel revolutions. Repeat rhythmically for a regular slub, regulating it according to the thickness and length required. A thick slub needs less twists to give it strength than is required of a fine length of thread. Combed locks or tops can also be used. Two colours can be introduced either in the rolag or by plying two slub singles together.

Fleck, nep or nub yarns

These are not precisely the same. A fleck is a felted nub of excessively short fibres, of a contrasting colour or colours to the base yarn, and incorporated in it at frequent intervals. A nub is similarly felted, but is of the same colour as the base yarn, and applied to it in the same way.

1 To prepare the nubs or flecks, heavily felt the required fleece by rigorous pounding in a soap lather.

2 Rinse and dry.

3 Cut it up into very small pieces.

4 Card the fibres for the base yarn, and sprinkle nubs over the card halfway through the process.

5 Spin a woollen or semi-woollen yarn. The nubs will remain within the yarn structure.

6 Wash the skein to assist cohesion.

Mixture yarns

These can have endless connotations from varying blends in carding and combing processes to a more textured appearance using unprepared locks from two different coloured fleeces more or less simultaneously. In this latter case take a lock of, say, natural black, and a white lock, both in the right hand. Spin as for a worsted type yarn, rocking the hand backwards and forwards intermittently to bring the two locks into greater or lesser play as required, but maintaining a tendency to a spiralling pepper and salt mixture and a slightly varied texture.

A semi-worsted yarn spun from locks, introducing occasional touches of colour, is most effective when strong bright colours are applied to the main background. The coloured fibres should be relatively short, and they should be prepared beforehand by combing, and the various colours laid out separately nearby. At regular intervals a few fibres should be introduced into the middle of the V of the drafting zone on the lock, and drawn into the yarn. The end result will depend on the quantity of coloured fibres applied and the overall size of the spun yarn. For example, if the locks are white, then pastel effects can be expected.

Textured yarns

Some of the most stable, satisfactory and sometimes most striking yarns are those completed by special plying methods. The following are a few of the possibilities.

Z spun thick and Z spun thin S plied
If each is held in a different hand a greater tension can be imposed on either the fine thread or the thick one, allowing the slack thread to spiral round the other. The tension can be reversed at short regular intervals to produce a third variation in type of yarn, and is further accentuated if each yarn is a different colour.

Slub yarns plied with fine singles
These are especially effective if the fine singles is spun in the same direction as the plying (e.g. fine singles S twist, slub singles Z, plied S). Two slubs of contrasting colour or fibre type can be plied to allow the slubs to overlap each other slightly and maintain a short length of finer two ply between the overlapped slubs.

Wrapped yarns
Usually known as knot yarns, several variations of wrapped yarns are possible. Two yarns of similar or contrasting type or colour are plied as follows. One yarn is held taut, whilst the twist is applied from the wheel in the usual way, and the other yarn is kept very slack. It is moved forwards and backwards to

allow it to spiral round several times and envelope the taut thread within lengths of about $\frac{1}{2}$ in (1.2 cm). These wrapped areas are arranged at regular intervals, and the two yarns can change roles if desired. Figure 125 shows how to use an improvised spindle wheel for this. A subsequent washing of the skein will prevent further slipping of the one along the other, if this is inclined to occur.

Conversely the ability to move the *spiralled* (wrapped) areas along the taut yarn may be an advantage on occasion, as for example when a concentration of textured surface is required in a woven hanging. A further development of this is achieved by using the wrapping yarn very firmly to build up a thickened area tapered to 1 in (2.5 cm) or more, with about 3 in (7 cm) of normal ply between each 'knot'.

Bouclé yarns
Bouclé or gimp-like yarns can be created by the use of one excessively high twist, fairly fine yarn, Z spun, and a medium twist yarn, S spun. During plying (Z plied) the two yarns are each held in a different hand, as in all the others just described. The hand holding the high twist yarn must be jerked forward slightly at frequent regular intervals to allow a short snarling of this yarn along the surface. If the initial twist and the overall control in plying is correct, it is possible to produce a small repeating loop snarl along the surface of the plied yarn. A longer snarl, more intermittently spaced is another variation on the theme.

9 *Skeining*

When the bobbin is full the yarn will need to be skeined off. There are only a few instances in which the yarn is wound direct onto a pirn for weaving, or a ball for knitting and crocheting, without further preparation. Normally skeining is required both for singles yarn and for plied, in order that the yarn may be washed and set and, in many cases, dyed as well. The usual method is to use a niddy noddy.

Using a niddy noddy

1 Remove the yarn from the orifice.

2 Slacken the bands on the wheel to the extent that there is a minimum of drag on the spindle and bobbin, but just sufficient to prevent the yarn from snarling up as it winds off.

3 Attach the yarn end to one arm of the niddy noddy.

66 Four different types of niddy noddies used for skeining

4 Grasp the centre of the shaft with the right hand and guide the yarn round the arms of the niddy noddy. As the name implies, this tool should rock backwards and forwards as if from an almost stationary pivot where the right hand holds it. Take the thread running from the attached position at the top down to and round the arm at the bottom, back to the top, round the arm on the other side of the shaft whilst giving the niddy noddy a quarter turn to facilitate this. Keep the grasp constant, but flex and bend the wrist.

5 Continue to carry the yarn down again and round the arm at the bottom (opposite side of shaft), and finally back up to the starting place, giving the necessary quarter turns. Repeat this movement until all the yarn is removed from the bobbin, or until a particular length has been wound off. The niddy noddy is sometimes made to allow about 2 in (5 cm) extra length on each 2 yd (2 m) span. This takes into account relaxation on the skein, when not at

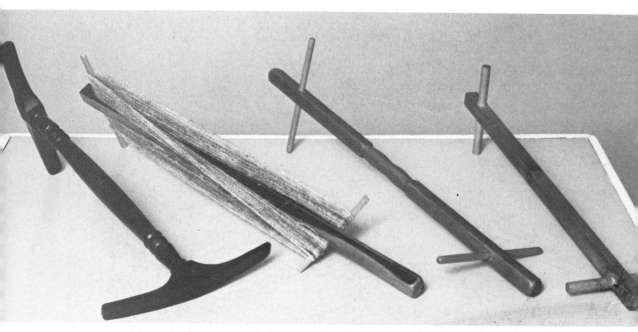

tension, plus the shrinkage caused by washing. The distance between the arms of the niddy noddy is normally 18 in (45 cm) from the outer edges, producing a 2 yd (2 m) skein. If the extra allowance is desired an extra 1 in (2.5 cm) must be added when making this piece of equipment.

6 Having completed the winding off, the end should be detached from the length of thread belonging to the bobbin or spindle, and tied *loosely* in a half hitch around the skein, and the knot completed. The beginning thread should be released and tied around the skein in a similar way. This ensures that either end can easily be found. Alternatively the beginning and end thread can be joined together. Note that it is often desirable when using yarns for knitting or crochet to start from the beginning end of the yarn. To ensure this, attach a short length of cotton thread to this end of each skein for identification.

7 The skein should have three further ties, especially if it is to be dyed. These can be of cotton or a reasonably strong 2 ply wool. Do not use dyed yarn for the ties, to avoid possible colour leakage on the skein during washing or dyeing processes. Use a figure-of-eight tie, by crossing the cotton yarn through the middle of the skein before tying the two ends securely together. They must be loose enough to allow even penetration in the washing (scouring) and dyeing stages.

Skeining around the hands

It is possible to skein off the yarn without a tool, namely between the two outstretched hands, but it is not easy to keep them constant in distance from each other. They should be held about 1 yd (1 m) apart, and moved backwards and forwards in such a way that the yarn winds around them. Start by wrapping the beginning thread securely round the thumb, and when the skein is complete, tie as described above.

Using a skein winder

A skein winder, or clock reel, turned by a handle, is occasionally obtainable, and is a quick and excellent way of winding off large quantities of yarn (figure 67). It is also easier to

67 On the left an antique clock reel skein winder, in the background a skein rack with washed skeins tensioned for setting (note the suspended weight on the lower bar), and on the right a two-band spinning wheel and a cloth finishing roller

measure the length as the winding proceeds (figure 68).

Washing skeins

If skeins have been spun from unwashed fleece it is advisable to soak them for some hours before proceeding with the washing. The extent of soaking will depend on the degree of dirt and grease present and the amount of twist in the yarn. It is important to avoid friction in the scouring process, as this can cause varying degrees of felting.

1 Using a galvanised bath or a sink for large quantities, a stainless steel or enamel bucket or bowl for smaller amounts, fill with sufficient lukewarm water to cover the skeins.

2 Immerse gently using minimum of movement. Leave several hours or overnight.

3 Remove and allow to drain. Immerse in clean water of same temperature.

4 Prepare a hand-hot scouring 'bath', using a gentle, high quality, liquid detergent (such as Teepol, Lissapol N, now called Synperonic N, or Stergene) – sufficient to maintain a moderate lather. Immerse the skeins and move them around squeezing gently if necessary and never rubbing. (A solution made from soap flakes, oil of eucalyptus and a little methylated spirits can be used where grease is very persistent.)

5 Lift them out and allow them to drain.

6 Prepare rinsing water at the same hand-hot temperature. Immerse the skeins and rinse with care.

7 Repeat stages 5 and 6 once or twice.

8 Hang the skeins along a strong clean bar. Insert a similar bar inside this line of skeins at the bottom. Gently even out each skein to eliminate kinks. Attach weights or improvised weights to the centre of the bar, or to the outer edges. This should be sufficient to straighten but not to stretch the skeins (figure 67).

9 Remove weights when dry.

68 Detail of the clock reel showing the ratchet mechanism, which registers yardage during winding

10 *Finishing processes*

The wool fibre

In order to understand the composition of woollen and worsted yarn and the fabrics from which they are made, it is essential to have some knowledge of the physical structure of the wool fibre. A study of the chemical properties under laboratory conditions would give the serious student a useful and more complete understanding of the fibre reactions to heat, acids, alkalies and much else.

The wool fibre, and indeed any hair fibre on the living animal, is composed of cells. Observation of a wool fibre under a microscope reveals an outer layer (termed a *cuticle*) consisting of overlapping scales. Each of these scales is a flattened cell, which projects slightly, pointing away from the root end of the fibre (figures 69, 70, 71).

The cellular structure beneath the scales is known as the *cortex*, and forms the main part of the fibre. Certain types of sheep produce a proportion of fibres which have a central air-filled core known as the *medulla*, and are sometimes referred to as hair fibres. They are often longer and coarser than the others. *Kemps* are short, whitish, brittle fibres which are shed into the fleece. They have an extremely large medulla, and therefore have little substance in them to take up dye. Usually they are to be avoided by hand spinners, but can be included in some tweeds to give a special and sometimes characteristic effect.

A magnification of a wool follicle would show the development and use of the sweat gland and the sebaceous gland (or wax gland). The greasy excretion from this latter coats the wool fibres before they reach the skin surface

69 *Left* Magnification (400 ×) of a Southdown wool fibre, **70** *centre* of a Shetland wool fibre and **71** *right* of an 80s Australian Merino wool fibre

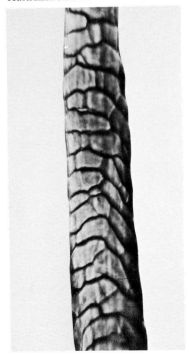
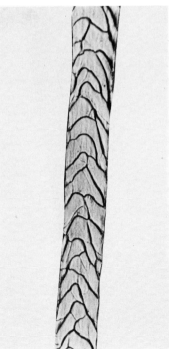

and renders the fleece on the animal water-proof. The combination of grease and sweat from the sweat gland sometimes results in a yellowish colorisation on the wool, which usually washes out.

The Mountain and Hill breeds of sheep some-times yield an outer coat of long coarse hair fibres and an undercoat of shorter, fine, woolly fibres. The Longwool sheep have less variation, whilst the Down breeds rarely have any. *Crimp* (i.e. small kinks along the fibres length) is present to a high degree in the Shortwool breeds. Longwools have little crimp in comparison but most have a distinct wave and a curly end to the lock.

Elasticity is one of the most valuable charac-teristics of the wool fibre. Due to this un-paralleled asset a woollen garment will regain its original shape after being worn some length of time. A wool fibre can be stretched under tension to one and a half times its original length. When released it will gradually return to its normal length within two or three days. This applies to the full if the scale structure has not been damaged by the use of harmful chemicals during any scouring, dyeing or finishing processes.

Cloth finishing processes

This is a field which is all too often neglected or only partially understood. It must be stressed that the cloth finishing process can be equally as vital as any other stage in fabric construction. Knitted and crocheted pieces must be properly finished too. The subject of this book is spinning, but the creation of yarn is not an end in itself. It is therefore of con-siderable importance to know something of the changes that are undergone before the woven length or knitted piece is in a fit con-dition for use.

Woven cloth finishes

When a mass of wool fibres is immersed in a solution of hot soapy water, the scales stand out from the fibre wall. If friction is applied, fibre movement results, the scales causing a

migration in the direction of the root end of each fibre. In due course, as friction is main-tained, the scales gradually close up again, and in doing so are inevitably caught up in scales of any adjacent or crossing fibres. These fibres are more or less permanently held together. This is how felting takes place.

In a woven fabric this combination of hot lather and prolonged overall and uniform friction causes a unifying of warp and weft threads in the weave structure and consequent shrinkage. It softens the woven *length* and turns it into a length of *cloth* or fabric. Fabrics need varying amounts of wet finishing, some actually requiring the opposite to felting, i.e. setting without shrinkage. The process known as *milling* or a *mill finish* can be either minimal or extensive, or any stage inbetween. Some wool fibre types have a far greater propensity to felt easily (this includes many of the Longwools), but it must be understood that a lightly spun yarn has greater potential for felting. This is due to the 'availability' of the majority of the fibres, to migration through friction, and attachment to other fibres. A high twist yarn allows of the outer fibres 'availability' (contact) only.

Milling

The normal method employed by hand spinners/weavers is, firstly, the initial scouring of the fabric to remove all grease, oil and dirt and subsequent rinsing, using hand-hot water in each case, and possibly prior soaking over-night if necessary. The woven length is then folded evenly to fit the bottom of the bath in which a high quality soap lather is ready, sufficient barely to cover the folded length. This is laid in and foot tramped until the required density (shrinkage) has been achieved.

Tweed lengths and other wool cloths intended for wearing apparel need sufficient felting to prevent loss of shape when worn (e.g. 'seat-ing'). A tweed-type upholstery length may need a firm finish if it is to withstand the wear required of it, but some types of cloth which are closely woven will need less heavy milling.

A useful test is to squeeze the excess moisture from a small area of the length, stretch it taut and draw a fingernail back and forth across the underside. If there is too much movement of warp or weft threads the fabric requires more tramping. The water temperature should not be allowed to drop too much and the lather must be maintained. Too much lather (i.e. a creamy consistency) would form a barrier over the fibres and prevent the necessary friction from being effective. Too little lather would not promote adequate movement of the scales.

The term widely used to describe a variation of this process is that of *fulling*, from which the name 'fuller's earth' derives, used as it was in the fulling mills in the west of England cloth manufacture during the last two centuries.

Tentering

The final process is to stretch the cloth to dry on a tentering frame, or on a cloth finishing roller as follows:

1 Place the roller on a clean table.

2 Cover with a cotton cloth stretched firmly (e.g. old sheeting). Put one end of the woven fabric spread centrally upon the last 12 in (30 cm) or so of the cotton cloth.

3 Begin to roll the roller forwards. Stretch the fabric sideways to create the maximum width from selvedge to selvedge and draw it forwards gently.

4 Roll forwards again about 4 in (10 cm).

5 Move the roller backwards across the table. Stretch the fabric firmly and evenly both sideways and forwards. Roll again another 4 in (10 cm). The tensioning of the cloth must be uniform throughout the proceedings and should be as taut as reasonably possible. It is a help to have two pairs of hands on the job, a person on each side to steady the roller and ease the cloth taut.

6 Repeat this to the end, and when fully rolled, a strong straight stick or bar (which can be covered with a layer of polythene if inclined to stain) should be placed along the edge

of the cloth and held in position with string or tape tied twice round the stick and on round the roller. Stand this upright in a dry atmosphere, reversing it occasionally to assist even drying out (figure 67).

Alternatively a tentering frame may be used.

Further finishing processes may be needed such as *raising the nap* with a loaded teazle frame, or a raising brush (figure 80). Small articles may be cloth finished in a similar way by hand squeezing (evenly) in a bowl of soapy water, until sufficiently felted, and rinsed in the usual way. They must be stretched out until dry by pinning them along the selvedges and ends to a cork bath mat or similar object.

Crabbing

Another process which is used in the finishing of woven fabrics is that of crabbing (or setting). This has the effect of preserving the weave structure as closely as possible to its appearance when on the loom. Little or no shrinkage or felting takes place in this process. If the weave is an open or lacy structure this textural character will be maintained throughout its life. If it is a comparatively closely structured cloth, the subtlety of the weave will remain clearly defined and clear cut.

The equipment required for a true crabbing process is a roller and a bath. The roller must be long enough to take the width of the woven piece plus 2 in (5 cm) or more extra on either end. The roller should be hollow, made up of a number of strong slats having approximately $\frac{1}{8}$ to $\frac{1}{4}$ in (3 to 6 mm) space between each, and with a diameter of not less than 6 in (15 cm). The bath, large sink or boiler must be large enough to take the roller. The size needed may present difficulties, but a shorter roller which will take the fabric folded in half lengthways may overcome the problem.

1 Wet out the length in warm water using the absolute minimum of handling.

2 Roll it onto the roller which has been previously covered with cotton cloth (old sheeting). Place a stick along the edge of the fabric to hold it in position and tie it on beyond the fabric selvedges.

3 Have ready a receptacle of water at 140°F (60°C), immerse the roller in it and rock it back and forth in this water for 10 minutes, maintaining the temperature throughout.

4 Lift it out and allow it to drain. Remove the fabric from the roller, replace it again, firmly stretched, and starting from the opposite end.

5 Have ready the receptacle containing boiling water, immerse the roller, and rock back and forth for 10 minutes maintaining a boiling temperature.

6 Lift it out, allow it to drain. Remove the fabric from the roller. It is now *set*.

7 Wash the fabric in the usual way, if necessary.

8 Finally stretch the fabric onto a dry roller covered with a cotton cloth (as described after the mill finish) and leave to dry. Subsequent washes will not alter the texture and character of the cloth provided the crabbing process has been done properly.

Steam pressing is an alternative method for smaller pieces, but great care is needed to avoid over-pressing and possible distortion of the length.

Blocking

Knitted and crocheted fabrics may require blocking, which entails stretching out the fabric over a flat surface with pins inserted round the edges to keep it taut and even, then holding a steam iron lightly on top of the surface to allow the steam to penetrate without pressing down on the fabric. The entire surface should be steamed, by picking up the iron and placing it down again, and never sliding it along. Alternatively a dry iron can be held on top of a damp cloth placed over the knitted piece. The fabric should remain stretched out until cool. The purpose of this is to flatten curled-in edges, and fix the shape of the stitches. Plain knitting requires blocking, but bulky fabrics and ribbing (as used for elastication) do not.

Part 2
Spinning with animal fibres

*Nature must be freely at work in
the mind when anything is well made.*
From *The Unknown Craftsman* by Soetsu Yanagi

11 *Silk*

Reeled silk

Silk yarn is produced in two distinct forms: reeled silk and spun silk. Reeled silk is a continuous filament which is wound or reeled from several cocoons at once to create a yarn composed of *x* denier (according to the number of cocoons incorporated). This is then normally plied, sometimes using six or more singles, and occasionally cabled (for braids and embroidery purposes). It is a specialised process, not normally produced by hand, except for experimental interest.

Sericulture

A brief description of *sericulture* (the rearing of silkworms) is appropriate here as most silk is obtained from the cultivated silkworm, *Bombyx mori*, though certain wild silks are obtained from silkworms living naturally on the mulberry trees and oak trees in China and other countries in the Far East (*Antheraea pernyi* is one of the wild varieties). *Tussah* is the term used for all Asiatic wild silk and is particularly attractive and suitable for hand spinning. *Raw* silk from the waste and damaged silk cocoons of the cultivated varieties is prepared into rovings and is obtainable in this form for hand spinning. It is usually white, smooth and extremely soft and lustrous.

The life cycle of the silkworm (a caterpillar of the *Bombyx mori* moth) begins with the laying of 300 or more small eggs, each the size of a pin head. Under suitable temperature conditions the eggs hatch into tiny caterpillars $\frac{1}{4}$ in (6 mm) long. These feed on mulberry leaves spread on trays. They grow rapidly, shedding their skins at intervals, and in about 5 to 6 weeks, when fully mature, they are approximately 3 in (7.5 cm) long and $\frac{3}{4}$ in (2 cm) in diameter, pale cream and almost transparent.

The mulberry on which they fed has been transformed into both liquid silk and sericin, a gummy substance.

Bundles of straw are placed near the edge of the trays. The silkworms climb up these (termed *The Rising*), anchor themselves with a few strands of thickish silk, and begin to make their cocoon around them. The caterpillar has two spinnerets in its head. The substances emerging from the sacs adhere, each solidifying on contact with the air. Its head moves in a figure-of-eight motion and the continuous filament builds up the wall of the cocoon layer upon layer, and this is made firm by the gum. The chrysalis then becomes dormant inside for several weeks before making a hole in the end and emerging as a moth. It mates, and the female lays eggs and dies within about 24 hours. Those concerned with sericulture must set aside a tiny percentage of the yield for this purpose, in cold storage.

Harvesting the silk

The main harvest of cocoons must be placed in special ovens at certain temperatures to stifle the chrysalis whilst dormant. The cocoons then remain whole. They are then reeled off in the following manner. A number of cocoons are floated in a bowl of boiling water to soften the gum. A large circular brush catches the outer silk area of the mass of cocoons, lifts them out and shakes them back into the water. In doing so the single filaments of each begins to unwind. A group of filaments and their cocoons (say 7) are transferred to another bowl of boiling water, these filaments are passed through a small hole, attached to a reel, which revolves, and a crisscross reeling begins. A 7 denier single silk filament is thereby formed and could be as much as $1\frac{1}{2}$ to 2 miles (2 to 3 km) in length.

Silk waste

There is a great deal of silk waste as a by-product of filament silk production and this can often be used for spinning, the different categories are as follows:

Floss – the outer hammock silk exuded on the Rising is a roughish silk used for spinning.

Frisson – is the first threads from the cocoon drawn off during the initial 'shaking down' process, and very strong.

Bassinets – is that composed from double, damaged cocoons and the inner endings of reeled cocoons, weaker.

Noils – the waste after degumming and combing (dressing).

Wild silk – as for example Tussah.

Degumming

Degumming is the removal of sericin and consequent softening of the silk. It is normally done in the raw state and the hand spinner may not need to perform this operation as most available silk is already processed. The slower method of degumming by a maceration process renders it more pliable and soft than the simpler boiling off procedure termed *discharging*, but modern developments have perfected the quicker process. Moreover the unattractive smell caused by maceration was difficult to remove even with bleaching in sodium peroxide.

For the amateur sericulturist the process of degumming is as follows. Soak overnight in soft, warm and slightly soapy water. Use rain water throughout if possible. Pour off the water and run soft warm water through it. Prepare a good soap solution (Lux or an olive oil based soap are recommended), immerse the silk and bring the water slowly to *below* boiling point, and simmer gently for an hour. Pour off and rinse in soft hot water.

If some of the gum is still present repeat the simmering and rinsing processes until com-pletely soft and pliable. To retain the natural lustre the liquor should never be allowed to boil. After the final rinse hang the raw silk up to dry in a warm place and away from direct sunlight.

Spinning silk

It is not always easy to obtain undressed raw silk, but the rovings are much easier to handle as they have already undergone a degumming process and the filaments have been cut into manageable lengths. These can be carded if desired. Tussah and other wild silks are creamy buff or honey in colour and only semi lustrous. These, and that of bassinet origin produce a somewhat uneven yarn but its softness and sheen gives it an attractive handle and appearance. They are obtainable in varying qualities.

Spinning from a roving
First method

1 Separate a length of roving of about 2 ft (60 cm) long into two or more slimmer lengths. Attach it to the yarn from the spindle by overlapping about 4 in (10 cm) and allowing the twist to join the end few fibres of the roving to the existing yarn.

2 Hold this join between the finger and thumb of the left hand and draw the sliver backwards with the right hand, letting a small amount of twist pass between the left hand, and draft further with the right hand.

3 Release tension and allow the thread to wind on. The process in this method requires sufficient tension from the spindle to draw out the fibres from the centre of the roving in a kind of 'sucking' action. The right hand must therefore maintain a light hold on the roving while the left hand should only operate intermittently to provide extra control. Sometimes it is necessary to even out the drafted thread with a slight unrolling movement. If this method is mastered it is both quick and satisfying.

Second method

1 Take a similar divided length of roving.

Fold it in half over the forefinger of the right hand. Join as usual.

2 Draft the fibres towards the orifice with the left hand, keeping a uniform V shape of fibres drawn from the fold.

3 Maintain a constant feed-in to the spindle to prevent overspinning. Treadle relatively slowly and work with a moderately tight band.

Spinning from a rolag and from carded blends

This can be done either in a semi-woollen spin, or in a long draw as for a woollen yarn or semi-worsted from carded silk rolled sideways across the carder. Silk does not have the resilience, elasticity and springy character of wool, but it is strong and reasonably durable. It also blends well with some wools and certain hair fibres. This blend is successfully achieved by mixing on the cards, but in certain circumstances a plying of one wool or soft hair fibre and one silk singles is both attractive and practical; cashmere and silk blend beautifully.

Skeining

In most instances handspun silk yarn can be wound direct onto a bobbin for weaving. If on the other hand some gum (sericin) is still present or it is to be dyed in the yarn, skeining is necessary. This can be done on a niddy noddy (see figure 66). For large quantities of very fine silk a clock reel with a yardage calculator is of great advantage. A criss-cross action should be employed in winding. The skeins must be carefully tied with four ties in a figure-of-eight tie repeated several times, using smooth silk or rayon cord.

Setting

Silk yarn intended for weft needs no further preparation. Yarn for warp will be stronger and smoother if *set*. This can be done by holding the skeins over a steaming saucepan for a minute or two then twisting them up tightly and hanging them between two rods in this twisted state in a cool place. Be sure to twist the skein in the same direction as the spin put into the yarn.

Characteristics of silk

Handspun silk yarn can be used in knit and crochet, but is more suited to woven structures. Garments and soft furnishings give scope for both exquisitely fine and more robustly textured silk and silk blend yarns. The main characteristics of silk yarns in use are as follows.

1 Silk cloth has an exquisitely soft handle and draping quality, dependent on the kind of silk and type of spin.

2 As a fibre it is relatively strong – though it is inclined to rot in time when subjected to adverse conditions.

3 Silk yarn combines well with wool and luxury hair fibres and sometimes with cotton.

4 It has reasonable elasticity, but less resilience than wool.

Finishing of silk fabrics

No wet finishing process is required unless the fabric is soiled. Steam iron pressing on the wrong side is best but pressure should be at an absolute minimum. Fair shrinkage of up to 3 in per yard (8 cm per metre) should be anticipated when calculating.

Dyeing

Silk takes natural dyes very beautifully but absorbs colour more mutedly than does wool. Acid dyestuffs are admirable for silk. Absolute boiling temperatures should be avoided if lustre is to be retained.

72 A stole made from hand spun silk, cashmere, alpaca and soay in natural colours

12 *Hair fibres*

Hair fibres shorn or combed from a wide variety of animals have undoubtedly been used for thousands of years and in various parts of the world, though primitive man has also sought to kill for pelts and hair-coated skins, thereby causing the near extinction of some species. (Sadly this is still occurring today.) Certainly the latter course has been a matter of necessity for peoples such as the Eskimos, Lapps and Tibetan shepherds, for example, but in general man soon came to the realisation that it was often better to pluck or shave off the annual growth and keep the animal alive,

and to utilise the yearly harvest of fibres to greater advantage by first spinning it and then weaving it or making felt fabric from it.

Many animals have a double coat, especially those living in high altitudes. It consists of a long, hairy, outer coat, and an ultra soft, short-stapled undercoat. These often have to be separated, and there is effective machinery in use in the hair fibre mills today for this purpose. In some instances, as for example with cashmere, the undercoat can be combed out carefully from the animal, leaving the outer coat unshed. It is an extremely slow process, and one Kashmir goat will rarely yield more than about 4 oz (112 g) of undercoat.

73 The border of a stole on the loom made from hand spun cashmere, alpaca, soay and silk, with a silk inlay

Most hair fibres are slippery, having very little crimp and little or no overlapping scale structure. Spin with a slackish drive band, but guard against overspinning. A fine mist spray of water (never oil) on rolags or locks can be applied during spinning if this proves to be beneficial, but experiment first. Hair fibre can be blended with wool in the combing process if it is too 'fly away'.

Cashmere

This can be obtained raw and scoured, or dehaired and in roving form. It comes from the Kashmir or Tibetan goat found in various parts of Asia Minor, Northern India and China. The undercoat is mainly white, but it can also be buff or pale grey (from China).

The roving or top should be divided in half or in thirds lengthwise, folded over the forefinger of the right hand, and drawn off from a V shape of fibres with the left hand (figure 74). It is a very slippery fibre, and practice and skill is required to strike a balance between overspinning and allowing the fibres to slip apart. Once a rhythm is achieved it should not be difficult to maintain this. It can also be spun without folding over the finger, holding the roving fairly lightly and moving the right hand outwards to its full length, paying out the fibres from the centre in a 'whistling' flow, and then allowing the length of resultant yarn to wind quickly onto the bobbin. In either case start the right hand about 9 in (23 cm) from the orifice of the spindle. If spindle spinning, use a lightweight spindle that spins freely, support it if necessary, and spin as described but using a vertical motion.

Camel

The short undercoat should be spun as for cashmere if it comes in roving form. If it is cleaned and dehaired but in a mass, a handful can be grasped and spun using a short V-shaped drafting action, treadling rather slowly at first, and having moderately tensioned bands to avoid overspinning. Carding gives better control, and is essential if blending it with other fibres.

Camel is sometimes obtained from zoological gardens or wild life parks, and is usually the moulted coat. It has a mixture of the soft undercoat and the other guard-hair fibres. It may need washing (as for wool), but vigorous treatment and consequent matting is to be avoided. Carding is necessary, and at this stage much of the hair fibres can be drawn off the card and put aside. The resultant yarn will be relatively wiry, and scratchy to wear.

Pure camel, spun from the undercoat only, is extremely soft and has a beautiful characteristic colour. It comes primarily from the Bactrian or two humped camel, whose habitat in parts of Asia exposes it to great extremes of temperature. The undercoat protects it from both, as is also the case with the Llama, Kashmir goat, the Musk Ox and many others. There are a number of different grades and qualities (and also degrees of under and outer coat) in the prepared mixtures that are available, and it is important to specify the quality desired when ordering from a hair fibre supplier.

Camel undercoat makes a very attractive blend with high quality Down fleece for use in fine knitting. It also blends with a well prepared Merino to produce a superb yarn. It must be carded with the wool fibres, and to obviate streakiness in the knit or weave accurate quantities of each must be applied to the carder and very evenly distributed. Camel will also blend with other hair fibres of similar staple length and character. The colour variation is one engaging feature if blending is only partial, but these variations need to be consistent throughout the article.

Alpaca

The animal thrives in high altitudes in South American countries, including Peru from where it originated. Related to the Llama, it is also of the camel species, as is the rare and much exploited Vicuna. Alpaca is a domesticated animal and is normally sheared. The

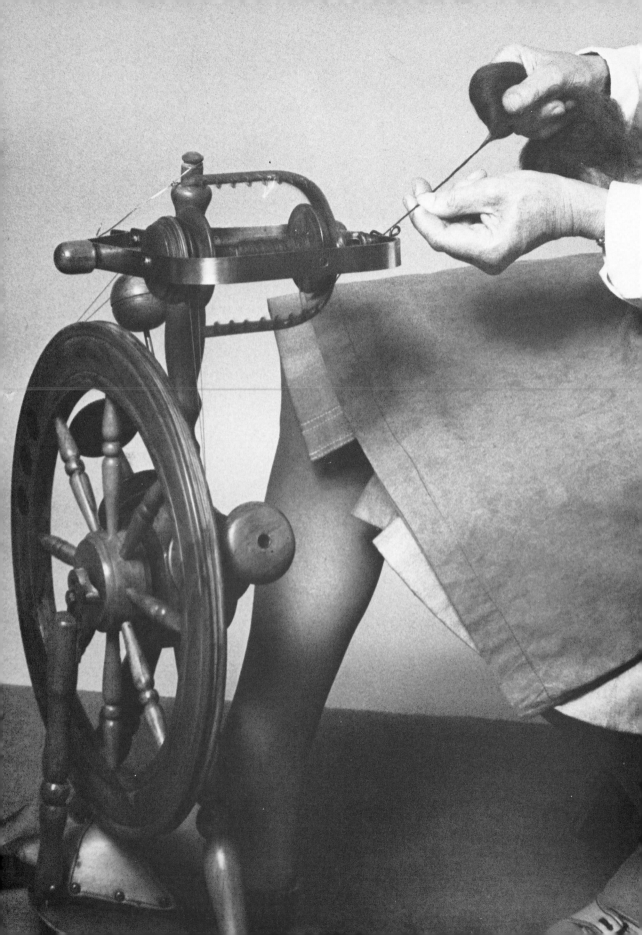

fibre has a longish staple, and it is the length combined with its strength that enables it to be spun into an extremely fine thread.

In roving form it is best folded and spun as described for cashmere (figure 74). If carded, it can be rolled crosswise and spun worsted fashion. Clasp the lock in the left hand and draft from the V shape in an even rhythm, whilst preventing the spin from running past the finger and thumb of the right hand.

The variations in the natural colours are surprising, mostly in red browns, they range from black to soft greys and pure white, and have differing degrees of lustre. If a whole 'fleece' is procured, gentle combing on the carders and a worsted type spin is advocated. This method helps to even out the colour.

As a 2 ply yarn it is admirably suitable for fairly loose knitwear and crocheted tops, and is very durable. Having no felting properties, it shrinks very little, but as with most hair fibres it is heavier than wool, and devoid of the resilient quality inherent in the latter. Additional warmth and softer handle to the fabric can be achieved by light brushing of the surface. This should be done whilst it is tensioned on a board.

Mohair

Mohair comes from the Angora goat. The goat originates from the Middle East, but it is now widely spread, being found in eastern parts of Europe, several extensive areas of the United States, and particularly in Southern African countries where large flocks are to be seen. This goat is about the size of one of the larger breeds of sheep, having a coat resembling the long, lustrous, curly Cotswold fleece. It is shorn and prepared for industrial usage in much the same manner as the Longwool breeds. If in roving form, it should be divided into 12 in (30 cm) lengths and spun from the fold. It is preferable to obtain raw mohair, so long as it is in good condition, and to comb or

74 Spinning alpaca with the top folded over the forefinger

card it. It is necessary to wash it first, and this should be thoroughly done. Mohair kid clippings are shorter, fine and lustrous, and have a beautiful handle.

Washing mohair

Soak it first in very hot water to release the dirt. Follow this stage with two hot soap lathers and several rinses, handling it very lightly at all times. Use plenty of water. A solution of washing soda (soda ash) at 2% induces a reduction in the grease content, but the mohair should not be left in the liquor for more than an hour. If very persistent, the addition of vinegar in the rinsing waters will help to lift the remaining dirt, and it also gives the mohair a good handle.

Some mohair retains a slight discolouration, and this part can be removed if a high lustre whiteness is required. Darker areas can be effectively used to produce a random shading effect, either undyed or top dyed.

Combing

This is necessary for long-fibre mohair when a fine, lightweight yarn is needed (as, for example, in light crocheted shawls).

1 Sort the fibres into qualities and keep them separate for all further processes.

2 Pull out the long hair fibres from the tips of the locks and set them aside.

3 Using a woolcomb having 2 or 3 rows of about 5 in (12 cm) long tines clamped to a table or bench, gently charge (load) it with the long fibres (butt ends on the tines and tip ends forward) until they are about 1 in (2.5 cm) from the top. Do not pack them down.

4 Draw off a small handful from the comb. Comb this over the tips of the tines, working gradually towards the centre, turning it over, and also reversing it from tip to butt end; comb through to the centre. When totally clean combed, lay aside. Draw off another handful and repeat. Continue until all the long fibres are combed. Remove the residue from the tines and recharge the comb.

93

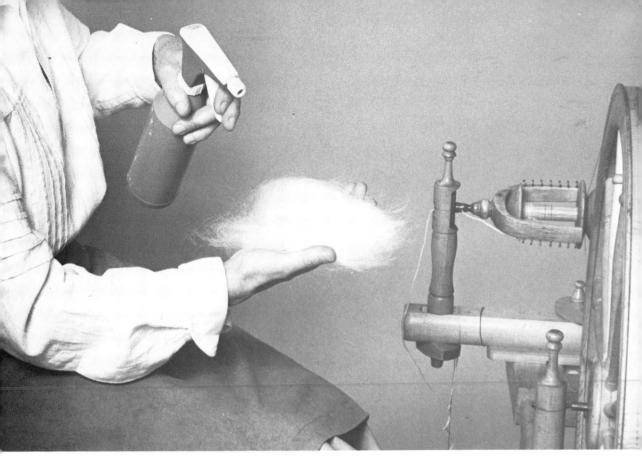

75 Spraying a combed lock of mohair with an atomizer   76 Drawing a thin film from the folded lock of mohair

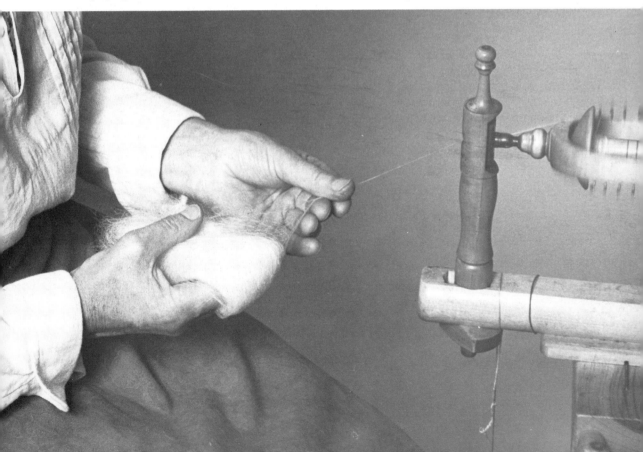

Spinning combed locks

To spin, spray the lock with a mist of water at 10% to 15% with an atomizer (figure 75). Lightly roll the combed lock, fold into a U shape, and spin semi-worsted fashion from a thin film drawn continuously from the middle of the U (figure 76). The yarn must be re-moved from the spindle immediately and the skeins lightly stretch–set whilst still damp.

A fine, light twist yarn can be used single or double (unplied) for lightweight crochet or knit, or for weft yarns.

Rough spinning carded fibres

The residue of short fibres from the combs can be teased, carded and semi-woollen spun. If somewhat matted, this can be partially teased and spun into a random slub yarn for various purposes, including a chunky knit. Delightful effects can be produced if some dyed mohair residue is mingled with some undyed, and rough spun into a multicoloured textured yarn.

Spinning mohair kid

Mohair kid is shorter stapled and softer than that obtained from the adult goat. If it is clean it will card with ease, and a very soft, silky, light, airy yarn can be spun from the rolags using a long draw, and taking care not to insert too much twist. The drive band should be fairly slack as is the case with most hair fibres, but a rapid feed-in is also needed. This shorter stapled type can also be rolled *across* the carder and handled as separate locks, drafting fairly extensively and rapidly, and feeding in quickly. A very fine, smooth yarn can be spun this way.

Heavy mohair yarn

A strong durable heavier yarn can be pro-duced for floor rugs, floor cushions, bags, etc. by teasing, carding and semi-worsted spin-ning, to excellent advantage.

77 *Right* Hand spun mohair floor rug from Lesoto (brown and gold bird motifs on a cream background)

Dyeing mohair

Mohair has a great affinity for dyes. Acid dyestuffs on mohair, used sensitively, produce most beautiful effects. The raising process commonly used in industry enhances the subtleties of the colours. Very smooth and exceedingly strong yarns are also a valuable attribute when a close texture and durability is the aim. Fibre ends, however, normally tend to protrude or become raised when friction is present, and this process occurs in everyday usage.

Raising the fibres of the yarn

A brushed or raised yarn can be made by dipping a hair brush in hot water and brushing it firmly down a skein which has been stret-ched and spread on a revolving floor swift (figure 80). It is essential to use water through-out this process to prevent disintegration of the yarn.

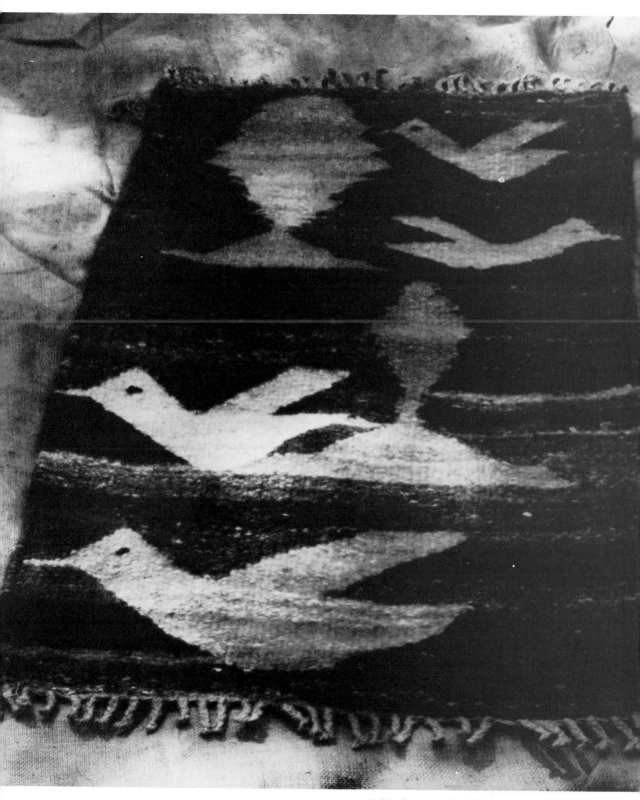

78 Hand spun mohair floor rug from Lesoto (white bird motifs on a dark blue background)

1 Spinning coloured and dyed fleece on a Saxony wheel

2 Natural coloured fleece and dyed fleece

Raising the nap of the fabric

Stretch the fabric on a board. Use a raising brush (similar to a small carder) or a hair brush, or a teazle-mounted brushing frame (figure 80) and gently apply with a slight drag and lifting motion. Work evenly back and forth over the whole piece. Normally one side only is treated.

Karakul

This animal is of the sheep family and is bred mainly in South Africa. The coarser and more wiry hair of this animal is to be obtained in the form of tops, and varies from cream to warm brown and charcoal grey. It should be spun similarly to most other rovings to produce a hard-wearing and slightly harsh yarn, mainly suitable for upholstery fabrics and floor rugs.

Goat hair

Goat hair is an all-embracing term used for the excessively coarse hair sometimes used by hand spinners, and produces a yarn of a wiry nature. Hard wearing in the extreme, it is suitable for floor coverings and (possibly) hangings. It should not be spun too finely as this is out of character with the raw material. Fairly slow treadling and a well tensioned band will prevent excessive twist.

Qiviut

This is an exquisitely soft and exceptionally lovely hair fibre. It is the undercoat of the rare species of ruminant bred in Alaska, commonly named Musk Ox. These delightful little animals are now protected, and increasing numbers of herds are being reared, though it is in the very limited areas of the cold Northern climes (principally in Canada) that they thrive. The undercoat, which is combed from them, is normally a smoky grey, and handles similarly to that of the finest cashmere.

79 Hand spun mohair floor rug from Lesoto (red and green bird motifs on a grey background)

Qiviut can be gently carded into rolags or spun from the soft mass held in the hand. A slack tension and rapid treadling is required. It should be spun fine, but careful adjustment of the wheel is needed to reach perfect quality of yarn. It is so precious that it would be sacrilege to combine it with lesser fibres, and should therefore be used for small and special articles, such as an attractive cap, or a cravat, or perhaps an openwork crocheted sleeveless top. Although it takes dye well, the natural colour is so unique that it is better preserved.

Angora rabbit

This is a relatively small animal yielding a very soft, lightweight fibre, either by plucking or shearing. The Angora rabbit's hair is extremely slippery to use and sheds somewhat both from the yarn and the finished article. It can be advantageous to blend it with a fine

97

wool, the angora hair producing a soft, fluffy surface.

Card it evenly with the wool and use a slack tension on the bands and a semi-worsted spinning method, but do not overspin. Wet out the skein and weight slightly to set it. It takes dyes well, but is more attractive in one of its natural shades, from white and soft greys to black.

The fibre length and diameter varies greatly according to the age of the rabbit and the area from which it is plucked. If it is to be spun on its own the fibres should be held in locks and worsted spun using a slackish band and adequate spin but without snarling. Very careful hand control and tension adjustment is needed.

Dog and cat hair

Both these have a somewhat limited appeal to spinners. However, there are those who derive singular pleasure from the challenge created by the immense range of hair types from both dogs and cats, and add ever increasing numbers to their collection.

Samoyed

The Samoyed may be considered to be in a special category, however the combings from these dogs is admirably suitable for spinning and highly satisfactory for wearing apparel (as when knitted or crocheted into garments). An important feature is that it should be combed regularly at the early time of moult (3 to 4 weeks) in order to extract the soft undercoat, *before* the longer coarser hair also moults.

After 'raising', it produces a full and fluffy surface not unlike a robust knit from an angora rabbit hair. Brushing over the surface of the completed garment to raise the hair is the accepted finishing process. Woven pieces, such as floor rugs, need not undergo this

80 In the background a mohair skein is being stretched on a revolving floor vice and brushed with a wetted hairbrush to raise the fibres; in the foreground a teazle frame is used to raise the nap of a knee rug while a log holds the fabric steady

treatment. The knitted article should be blocked at the time of raising. A bristle hair brush is recommended and the surface worked over systematically from top to bottom. It is preferable to 2-ply the yarn for knitting, and sufficient initial spin must be given to the singles yarn to allow for this.

To prepare the hair, tease if necessary, card into rolags, using a very light carding action. Spin as for wool, drafting freely to arm's length. For knitted garments a light, air-filled yarn is needed. It is important to experiment to get the right tension. If the yarn is to be plied, the twist on the singles should be adjusted to allow for this. Samoyed takes dye beautifully, but requires a longer time in the dye bath than wool.

Afghan Hound

Although Afghan hair is rather silkier and longer than Samoyed, it can be prepared and handled similarly. The combings are a light camel colour, and produce a soft and fluffy haloed surface to the yarn. It is suitable for wearing apparel and other uses.

Old English Sheep Dog

Combings from this breed yields a lovely mixture of colours from soft silvery greys to whites, and has a pleasant handle. It is not quite so fine as that of the Samoyed nor does it 'raise' so perfectly, nevertheless it can be prepared and spun similarly.

Airdale Terrier

This hair has a shorter and wirier staple, but it spins well from closely rolled rolags.

Deerhound

This is a less commonly obtainable combing, but will spin satisfactorily if handled as for Samoyed.

Poodle

Poodle clippings are short, curly and slippery to spin. They are more controllable if blended

81 Spinning Samoyed dog hair

with a small quantity of short-stapled wool fleece. A Southdown fleece is suitable for this purpose.

Other breeds

Many more breeds of dogs yield combings that will spin a usable yarn. In almost all cases it is better to card to produce as close a rolag as practical. Most dog hair blends well with a fleece whose staple length and character is akin to it, and as the slippery tendencies are dimin-

ished spinning tends to be easier. It should not contain more than 50% wool.

Cat

Combings from long-haired cats are incomparably soft and fly-away, and difficulties can be experienced through the added complication of static electricity. It should be carded as follows: place the fibres evenly across the carder; dampen slightly; card extremely lightly; remove each layer separately and roll firmly across the back of the card. Spin as for angora.

Part 3
Spinning with vegetable fibres

*The material provided by nature is nearly
always best. Nothing is more precious than
the unspoiled character of raw material . . .
The closer we are to nature (in crafts) the safer
we are.*
From *The Unknown Craftsman* by Soetsu Yanagi

13 *Flax*

Processing fibre flax
Types of flax

There are two types of line flax (*Linum usitatissimum*), one being termed fibre flax, and the other seed flax (also referred to as oil flax or linseed). A dual purpose flax is also grown. All fibre flax cultivated today derives directly from that grown in the Baltic in earliest times. Varieties and qualities of this annual self-fertilising plant are numerous. The fibre flax varieties grow up to about 48 in (120 cm) tall, and are found in more temperate climates in the northern hemisphere. Russia is an important flax producing area, while Belgium and the Netherlands grow the finest quality. Linseed varieties are branched up the stem, which is shorter and the seeds are much larger than those of fibre flax. Warmer regions of the world, such as Argentina, India, Uruguay, and parts of the USA, Canada and the USSR cultivate this type.

82 Flax fibres under magnification

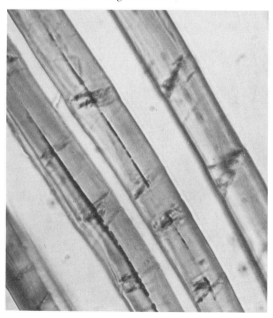

Cultivation of fibre flax

Fibre flax needs ample rainfall and temperate conditions when growing, and the closer the seed is sown, the smaller the stem and the finer the quality of fibre bundles within it. Sowing up to 3000 plants per square metre (per square 39 in) is the norm in France and Belgium.

Small areas of flax can be cultivated for experimental purposes by individual hand spinners. It is desirable to sow early (late February to early April) to prevent too rapid growth in the early stages, which would produce weak plants. As the finer quality fibres are found within thin stems, the seed should be sown thickly to encourage this. Rich, slightly acid soils are best and not too exposed conditions. Flax plants should be kept free of weeds.

Harvesting

The root of the fibre plant is very short and thin, and contains the ends of the fibres. Therefore harvesting is done by *pulling* (not by cutting) in order to obtain the full length of the fibres and maintain its quality. Harvesting for line flax needs to take place before maturity, i.e. when the lower two thirds of the stem has turned yellow. Fibres from fully matured flax are both stiffer and coarser. The time for pulling varies, according to conditions, from July to September. After pulling, the flax should be tied in convenient bundles and left on the ground for several days to dry before removing the seed. This deseeding process is known as *rippling*.

Rippling

Rippling by hand is effected by drawing the heads of the flax bundles through a line of long sharp pointed nails protruding vertically from a board which is clamped to a bench. The seed released by this method is immature and

therefore not suitable for resowing. The flax is then retied in bundles and stood in stooks for up to a week, to complete drying.

Retting

There are several forms of retting: dew retting, pond retting and tank retting. Sometimes a combination of processes is employed. The retting function is that of separating the fibres from each other and from the outer stem and inner woody core. It is a natural fermentation process which causes decomposition of an adhesive substance. The action of the micro-organisms is apparent when the yellow stems turn to a reddish brown through to grey, and under ideal conditions, to a blue grey. In all cases frequent inspection is required during retting to avoid impairing the quality of the fibre.

Dew retting

Dew retting is most effective in damp weather and can take up to eight weeks. During a dry

83 Harvesting flax

period the flax must be kept damp by watering. The flax is spread out on the grass and occasionally turned over.

Pond retting

Pond retting, or stagnant water retting, is speedier, due to organic matter present which assists the fermentations, but there is a danger of over retting. The flax is subsequently spread out thinly in the open for about a week. The process is called *grassing*, the sun, rain and air completing the removal of the adhesive substances.

Running water or river retting is safer, and is a method long practised in Belgium. The bundles of flax are packed in wooden straw-lined crates. These are submerged vertically, anchored and weighted just below the surface and kept submerged for from ten to twenty days, dependent on the temperature of the water.

Tank retting

Tank retting is a relatively artificial method, the crates being loaded into tanks through which water slowly runs.

Hand spinner's method of retting

The bundles are usually steeped in water for about a week, and the retting is completed by the dew retting process. Warm weather conditions accelerate the process. Testing is done by breaking a flax stem near the base; the woody exterior should fall away. The flax bundles may be dried and stored until such time as they are required for further processing.

Breaking

Breaking (or beetling), as the name implies, breaks up the woody exterior and centre core and facilitates the removal of these parts from the fibres. Originally wooden mallets were

84 Scutching flax by hand on a scutching stock (County Antrim, Ireland)

used for this, until the development of bladed breakers mounted on stands. In Ireland a stone wheel, drawn by a horse, was used to break or bruise the flax prior to scutching.

Scutching

A scutching blade is used down the side of a broad upright board as the flax bundle is gradually moved forward across the top. The blade beats away the woody particles which drop away and leave the fibre bundles (figure 84). This process also begins to separate the fibre bundles. There is a certain amount of wastage in the form of broken fibres, known as *tow*, which can be used to make a rough spun yarn. (Harvesting, scutching and hackling are here illustrated as practised in Ireland at the turn of the century.)

Hackling

This is a combing process which further divides the bundles of fibres until they are as fine as the flax quality allows. It also completes the

removal of woody particles still adhering. Hackling combs (figures 85 and 86) (whether hand operated or for commercial usage) are made in a series of four or five from coarse through to very fine. The teeth are set in rows of pointed metal tines, each with a different setting. When each bundle or strick has been through all the combs in turn it should appear soft and lustrous and the fibres should be fine and uniform. The colour varies according to the variety and the harvesting and retting conditions. *Tow flax* is that remaining in the combs, tangled and with short broken fibres.

Whether the processes described above are handled commercially or by hand, as our forebears have done, the methods of preparation are fundamentally the same. The hand spinner will require line flax in well hackled 'locks', termed *stricks* (or sometimes *heads*) before quality spinning can begin. On a coarse, incompletely hackled strick a metal dog comb can be used if the strick is held firmly at the centre, and the comb moved up each time as combing proceeds, then, reversing the strick, combing should be similarly done from the root end to the centre.

Preparing the flax for spinning

This is the stage at which most hand spinners begin to handle the raw material. To spin flax fibre, it is necessary to bind it to a distaff (a tall wooden pole) so that the bottom of the flax is at hand height.

The distaff

A free-standing distaff is preferable to one mounted on the spinning wheel in most cases, as it gives greater freedom for positioning it in relation to the orifice on the wheel. Distaffs throughout history have often been either wonderfully carved, inlaid, elaborately turned or even ornately painted, according to their source, but a simple strong straight post, having a groove at the top, and mounted firmly on a broad heavy log as a base is equally

85 Hackling – a rougher at work in an Irish mill

functional provided the height is right, approximately 4 ft (1.2 m) from head to floor.

Distaffs vary in shape, some are built in a conical shape, some in a lantern-like form. If it is a turned wood upright, or even a broom handle(!), it is desirable to attach a cone-shaped form in soft paper, smoothly covered in a shaped single sheet of paper, or else a cardboard cone. This should be firmly attached to the distaff head.

Binding the strick to the distaff with a ribbon is known as 'dressing the distaff' or 'dressing the dolly'. This may be done in several ways, and three methods are given below, the first of which requires the strick to be cross combed into a fan shape.

Cross combing

This is probably the most common method in use today, and is generally considered the easiest in the production of fine uniform yarn. Moreover, the distaff, in this case, need not be excessively tall. Flax fibres are between 25 in

86 Hackling on a board gripped between the knees (County Antrim, Ireland)

(60 cm) and 35 in (90 cm) long, and the overlapping of them in a criss-cross manner enables the spinner to draw them out in a uniform flow with relative ease, as spinning proceeds. It is of the utmost importance that the following procedure is adhered to carefully.

1 Take a strick in the hand, hold it firmly by the root end and give it a sharp shake in order to release the fibres from their compact state.

2 Tie the centre of a 3 yd (3 m) length of smooth ribbon, approximately $\frac{3}{4}$ in (2 cm) in width, tightly around the top of the strick about 3 in (7 cm) below the root end.

3 Wearing a smooth, flat cotton apron and seated on an upright chair with knees wide apart, tie the ribbon around the waist with the flax attached in the centre front. The intention is to produce a fine fan-shaped film of criss-crossing fibres, layer upon layer.

4 Begin at the extreme left, holding the strick

near its lower end in the right hand in a pincer-like hold between straight fingers and thumb. With the palm of the left hand detain a thin film of fibres (figure 87). Move the strick fan-wise across the lap paying out a fine film which is controlled by the left hand palm downwards, also moving across (figure 88).

5 When a complete open fan-shape is achieved, fold the slightly diminished strick over carefully and transfer to the left hand (figure 89).

6 Repeat the process in reverse, creating a second layer. Continue backwards and forwards in this way (executing the utmost care), layer upon layer, until all the flax is spread.

7 Untie the ribbon at the back of the waist. Gently lift the 'fan' onto a flat surface. Turn up the lower edge about 2 in (5 cm) and press firmly against the main area (figure 90). This ensures that all straggling fibres are tucked inside. The flax is now ready for dressing the distaff.

Dressing the distaff after cross combing

1 Lay the distaff (top section) along the centre of the fan. Tie the ribbon very firmly around the top.

2 Swathe the fan around and allow it to overlap on itself. See that it is firmly held together and then tidy the flax tips at the distaff head arranging them to stand up freely.

3 Placing the distaff upright in its holder, take each end of the ribbon round and round the cone of flax in opposite directions and finally tie it in a bow at the base.

Alternatively the distaff may be dressed upright (figures 91, 92, 93). Remember that when spinning a fine thread in particular, the flax is more easily controlled by the spinner if it is tied onto the distaff as firmly as possible.

Dressing the distaff without cross combing

In this case the distaff must be taller than that used for the fan-shaped method.

1 Give the strick a sharp flick from both ends.

2 Ease the top round the head of the upright distaff and tie it very firmly with the ribbon.

3 Criss-cross the ribbon around it several times and tie in a bow at the bottom (figure 95).

It is sometimes considered an advantage to a further control of the flax fibres in spinning if the strick previously is folded back and forth across its length in pleats approximately 2 in (5 cm) wide, and left some hours under pressure. It maintains a wave when shaken, and is then attached to the distaff as described.

Dressing the distaff with a U-shaped strick

1 Fold the strick in half, U-shaped, and lay it on a table.

2 Ease a few fibres forward by grasping a small number from the centre area of the U shape.

3 Place the distaff pole to lie at right angles to the fibres, and roll these first few fibres round it.

4 Ease a few more and draw them outwards with the distaff and roll on a little. Repeat this gradually until all the fibres have been rolled onto the distaff in a thin, even film. The flax is now ready for spinning when the distaff stands in position.

The water pot

Line flax is normally spun wet, so it is necessary to fill a small bowl with water and place it on a stool so that the fingers can be frequently wetted. Some spinning wheels have a water pot built onto the design (figure 117). Ordinary water is suitable, or a solution may be made by pouring hot water onto a handful of Carrageen Moss, as this strengthens the flax for weaving. Saliva is also effective, as used by the spindle spinners in Egypt.

Spinning flax
Wheel spinning from cross-combed flax

A freestanding distaff should be on the spinner's left in line with the chair and almost opposite the orifice. A stool beside it should

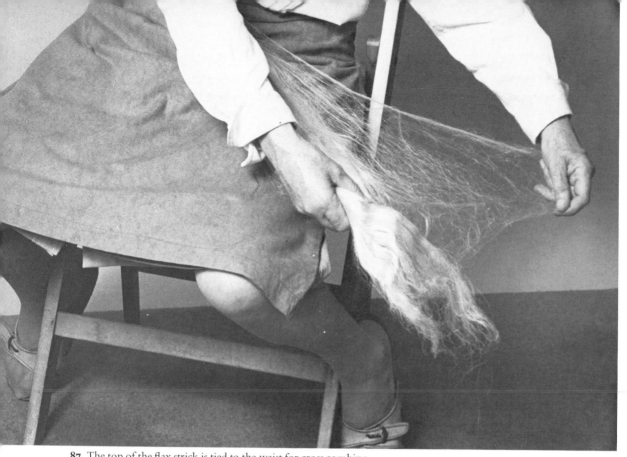

87 The top of the flax strick is tied to the waist for cross combing
88 Completing a single film of the fan

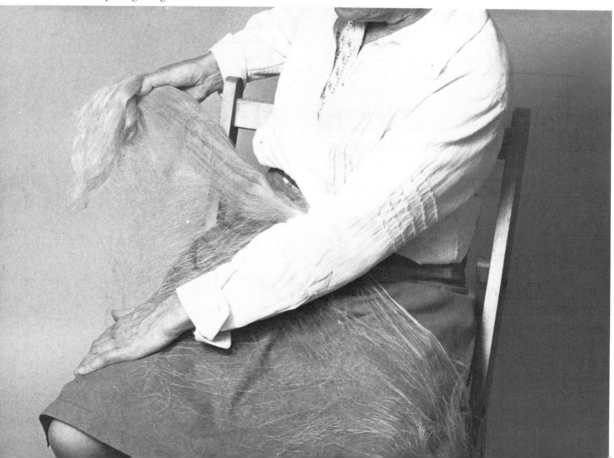

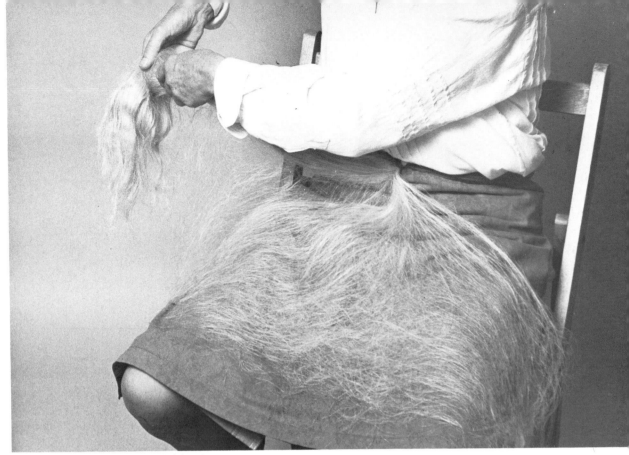

89 Transferring the strick to the left hand
90 Folding back the bottom edge of the completed fan

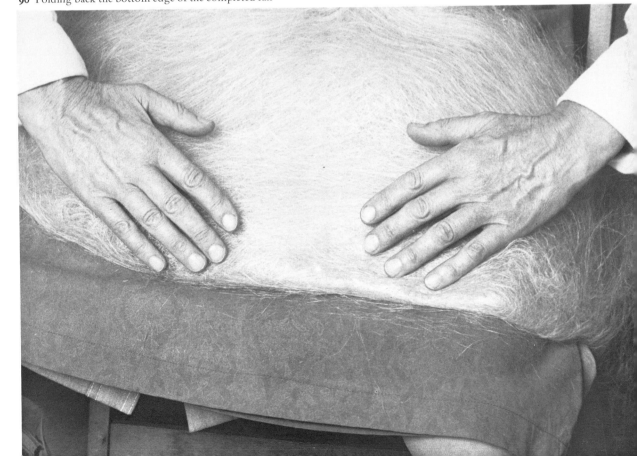

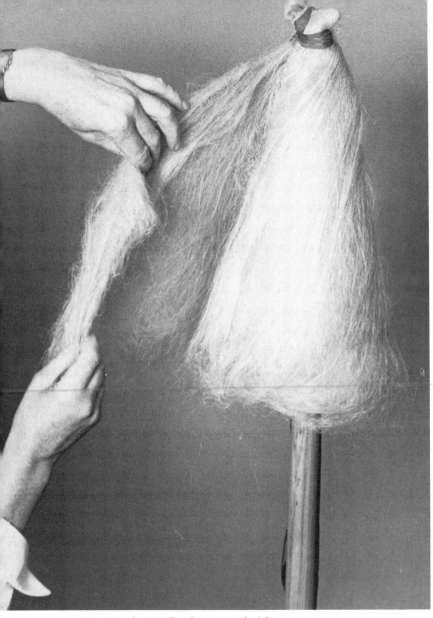

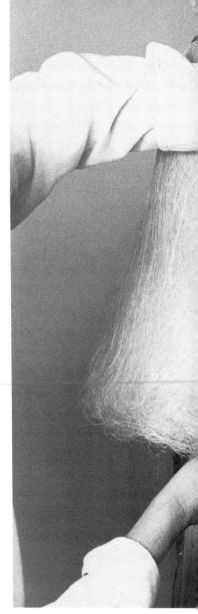

91 Dressing the distaff with cross combed flax

92 Swathing the fan round the cone

hold the bowl of water. A length of cotton or linen yarn attached to the empty bobbin and protruding through the orifice should be dampened between wetted finger and thumb and laid at an angle across the dressed flax.

With the wheel rotating and an average tension on the bands, take this thread between the wetted finger and thumb of the left hand, rolling it gently backwards and forwards between them, and draw downwards towards the orifice. This will cause a number of fibres to attach themselves to the thread. Spinning has commenced (figure 94).

The art of producing a fine and even linen yarn is achieved by a combination of even rhythmic movement, even drafting and the skill of keeping a uniform supply of overlapping fibres moving into the yarn throughout the proceedings. Once this rhythm and control is acquired and the distaff is well dressed with quality flax, the creation of good linen yarn is comparatively easy. Sufficient twist is of paramount importance, but over twisting must be avoided. A very lightly spun linen yarn is rarely acceptable for any purpose.

The left hand does virtually all the work but

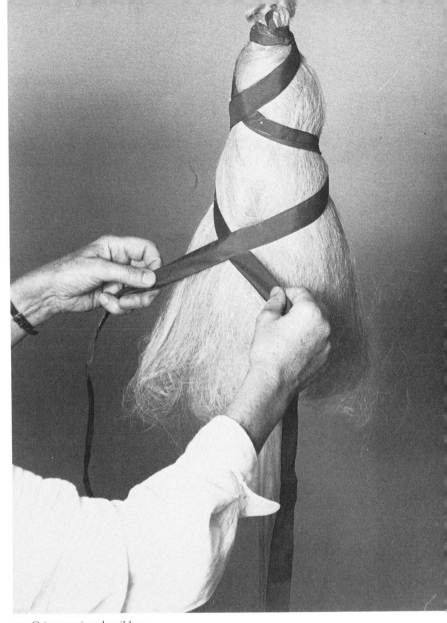

93 Criss-crossing the ribbon

each time a wetting of the fingers is required the right hand can be used to prevent the twist running up and so collecting extra fibres. Should the yarn tend to become too thin the left finger and thumb should roll the yarn back and forth between them more vigorously as it moves upwards towards the distaff, thus collecting more fibres. The drafting motion is a forward one, and the range is up to approximately 12 in (30 cm) ending 2 to 3 in (5 to 7 cm) from the orifice.

As the dampened left hand finger and thumb are moved backwards along the newly spun

stretch they have the essential role of smoothing the thread, thus preventing the protrusion of fibre ends. This is very important. If too many fibres become involved or too much twist runs up into the flax, the wheel should temporarily be stopped, the left hand should take out the twist by an unrolling of the thread between finger and thumb in this region, and then take a longer draft in order to thin out the offending area.

The right hand finger can occasionally be used in a comb-like fashion to ease the excess fibres *backwards* and upwards, but too much use of

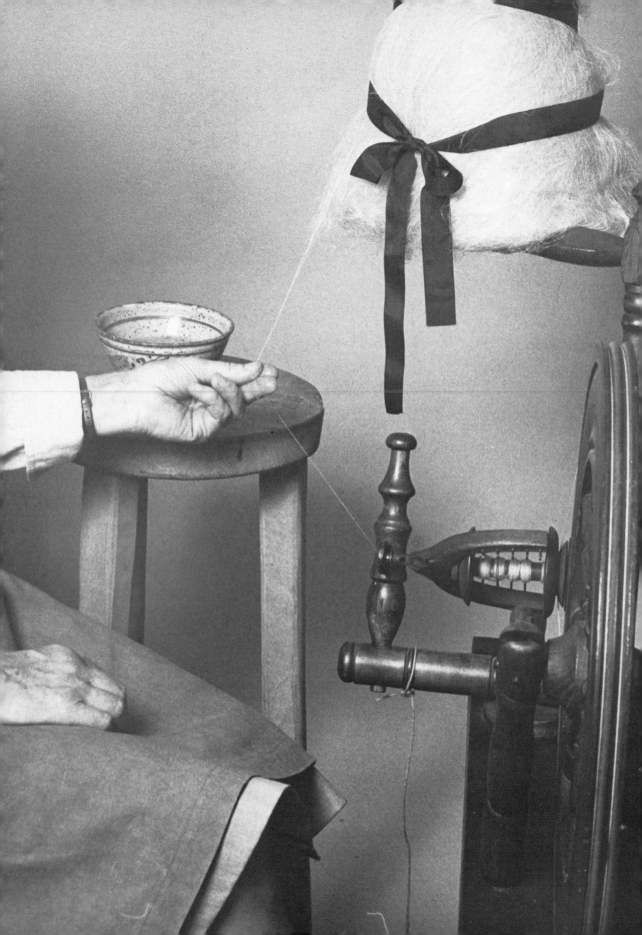

the right hand is undesirable. If the distaff preparation has not been perfect the fibres may get out of hand. Fold straggling ones firmly back underneath and resume spinning from a fresh position.

It is important to remember to move the yarn back and forth along the flyer hooks very frequently to prevent excessive build up in one area of the bobbin. Transfer to several hooks away from the previous one, so that the yarn is wound on obliquely. This obviates the risk of losing the end in the event of a break. As the dressed flax reduces, the ribbon may need re-tying from time to time. It is possible to move the dressed flax round at intervals to achieve an even usage by persuading fibres on the left of the drafting area to be incorporated, whilst relinquishing a few on the right. The distaff may need to be turned manually to facilitate this.

It is the fibre quality and end usage which dictate the yarn size (thickness). A coarse or poor quality fibre will not make a satisfactorily fine yarn. The amount of twist and the size of yarn must be determined when the character of the flax is established.

94 *Left* Spinning the flax with wetted fingers; here the distaff is mounted on the wheel
95 *Below* On the left, spinning from cross-combed flax, on the right, spinning from non-cross-combed flax

Wheel spinning from non-cross-combed flax

The distaff should stand on the spinner's left with the water bowl beside it (figure 95). A few fibres are twisted onto the yarn protruding from the orifice, and spinning commences as given above. The drafting requires a great deal of care and skill to prevent it from collecting too many fibres at once. The fibres must be staggered to overlap intermittently, and if this is attained an excellent yarn may result.

Spinning tow flax

Tow flax can sometimes be obtained in roving

96 Spindle spinning flax from a distaff

97 Controlling the twist with the left hand

form, and if spun as such can become an attractive, rough-textured yarn. It can alternatively be combed after a fashion to render it more controllable, and being fairly short stapled can be spindle spun more easily than line flax. There are distaffs designed to hold rovings of tow flax (known as tow forks) but if desired, combed or hackled rovings can be wound into a ball (or onto a large spool), placed in a box or bowl, and spun using both hands and a forward drafting rhythm. Wet spinning is not always used in the making of tow flax yarn; it is a matter of preference. Beware of over-spinning.

Spindle spinning with dressed flax

This skill is not commonly practised, but is not particularly difficult. The spinner should be seated with the distaff and bowl of water standing to the left side. After joining as described in the wheel spinning method, the rolling actions and drafting method are as for wheel spinning. The right hand must maintain sufficient rotation of the spindle, and when winding the yarn onto the spindle base care must be taken to prevent twist running past the thumb and finger of the left hand and into the fibre mass on the distaff (figures 96 and 97).

Finishing processes for linen cloth

The finishing processes for linen should be considered when designing the yarn. Many attractive fabrics are produced using a combination of bleached and unbleached linen. Half bleaching also has a place, and dyeing too. Dyeing is more satisfactory on bleached linen yarn, which absorbs the dye more readily. The final process which gives the linen cloth its most perfect pristine finish is pressing and polishing, described below.

Bleaching
Grass bleaching
The safest and best method for the handspinner to employ is perhaps that which is known as *grass bleaching*. It is probably the oldest and most widely used method. *Grassing* is a slow

process, but gentle, and not liable to cause damage to the fibre structure. Moreover being a natural process it is complete and permanent.

The skein of yarn, or the fabric, is simply laid out on the grass for several weeks, during which time the colour present in the fibre is gradually removed by the oxygen given off by the plants and from the atmosphere. The linen gradually whitens and is eventually totally bleached. It should be kept damp throughout the processing. Some protection from staining or damage may prove necessary and occasional turning over speeds up the process.

Chemical bleaching
There are several methods used, each containing the essential ingredient of chloride of lime. Prior to any bleaching process the linen yarn or fabric should be boiled in a good quality soap solution for approximately an hour, rinsed, and then boiled again in a similar solution. If lime alone is to be used it should be dissolved in rain water (if possible) at the rate of 2 oz (56 g) of chloride of lime to 2 pints (1 litre) of water. This is the *concentrated* solution, and great care must be taken in its use.

Make a bath of sufficient liquid to ensure adequate coverage of the linen, in the proportion of $\frac{1}{2}$ pint (0.25 litre) of the concentrated solution to 8 pints (4 litres) of water, a 16:1 ratio. Immerse the linen and keep it totally submerged for 2 to 3 hours, turning it occasionally using a glass rod. Lift it out and expose it to the air for several hours. The lime-absorbed fibre has a great affinity to the oxygen in both the air and water, and the released oxygen destroys the colour in the fibre. If one application of this process is insufficient it may be repeated. Finally the bleached linen should be washed and dried in the open air.

Some bleaching agents include potassium permanganate, hydrogen peroxide and potassium aluminumate in addition to chloride of lime. They all contain a high degree of oxygen which when released attacks the colouring matter in the linen fibre, and other unbleached materials. Most proprietary makes are safe.

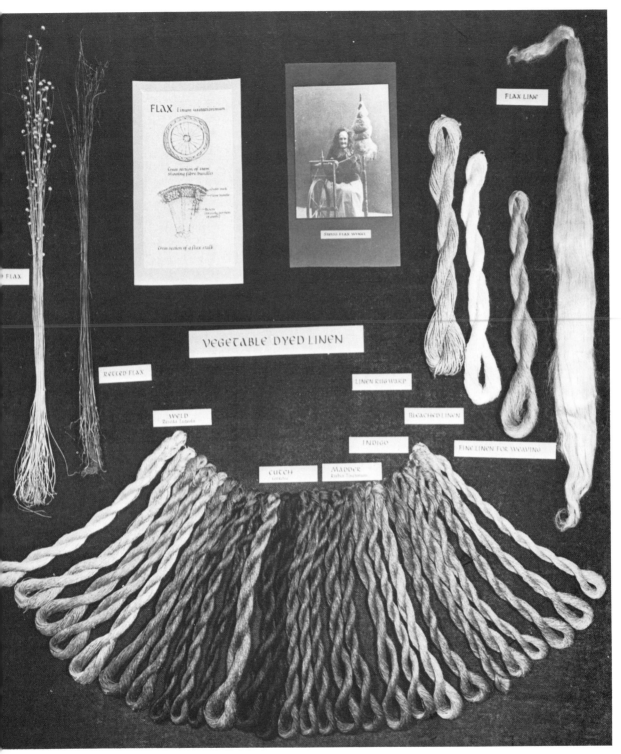

Labels visible in the display image:

FLAX

FLAX *Linum usitatissimum*

Swiss Flax Wheel

FLAX LINE

VEGETABLE DYED LINEN

RETTED FLAX

LINEN RUG WARP

WELD
Reseda luteola

BLEACHED LINEN

INDIGO

FINE LINEN FOR WEAVING

CUTCH
Catechu

MADDER
Rubia Tinctorum

98 A display of flax and linen (from left to right): pulled flax (before rippling), retted flax, cross section of flax fibre, a Swiss flax wheel, three skeins of unbleached, bleached and plied yarns, a strick ready for spinning; (below) a range of hand spun, vegetable dyed skeins.

Gold bleaching

Gold bleaching is effected by boiling the linen in a solution of soap and soda. Use in the proportion of 1 oz (14 g) of soap and 1 oz (14 g) of soda to 1 gallon (4.5 litres) of water. Prepare the solution, immerse the linen (which has been previously wetted out) in it, and bring it slowly to the boil. Simmer for about 2 hours. Leave the linen immersed for about 24 hours. Repeat the whole process if necessary up to three applications.

Dyeing

Linen is very beautiful whether in its natural state, bleached or half bleached. Though endowed with less affinity to dye pigments than many fibres, it nevertheless takes on a very lovely quality of its own. Natural dyes such as indigo, madder, weld, walnut, cochineal and many others, give linen special tonal subtleties peculiar to it alone. Good mordanting and adequate quantities are essential. In the chemical dye range, direct dyes are most suitable for the hand spinner.

Finishing

No hard and fast rules need be adhered to in the finishing of linen fabrics, but certain guidelines are useful. It is important to know that a linen yarn, though round when spun, changes its shape more or less permanently when pressed. For example, a fabric which shows a space between each thread whilst being woven will have those spaces closed when it is steam pressed or ironed, due to the flattening and consequent spreading of each yarn, both in the warp and the weft. In addition, linen has a natural sheen, and this may be enhanced by what is known as *polishing*. The use of a damp cloth or steam iron, and careful ironing from side to side (taking the utmost care to preserve the shape), will initially flatten the yarns, and subsequently give the fabric the characteristic polish found in the highest quality industrial finishes. Normal laundering when the article is in general use eventually achieves this anyway.

Alternatively it can also be argued that a light press on the wrong side only is the preferable and more authentic way to present a hand woven piece.

Crocheted linen and linen lace should *not* be pressed. This should be stretched (pinned) out on a board. A light steaming may help to set it.

In all instances it should be remembered that a wetting process can result in some release of the natural colour, and staining may occur in some areas of the material.

Suggestions for the use of linen yarns

The use of the linen yarn is naturally dependent to some extent on the quality of fibre available. Pure linen fabric inevitably creases readily and is better suited to table linen and furnishings than to wearing apparel. Its cool feel, however, makes it attractive to wear in very hot weather, and a sleeveless top is a suitable simple garment to make from it.

Hand spun linen yarn can also be used in lace making and in crocheting, but needs to be fine and with a good degree of twist and uniformity. Hand spun linen fabric can be designed and woven as a base for embroidery, while hand spun linen yarn can be designed for use as an embroidery thread. It also has a special place in purely decorative use in *woven hangings*. The yarn can be used as weft on a cotton warp, but its total lack of elasticity makes it impractical for it to be used in connection with cotton and other yarns in the warp alone, or the weft alone (except on rare occasions for special effects).

Plying renders linen stronger, and this sometimes makes it more suitable for warps. Tow flax produces a rougher, more fibrous character of yarn, and can be used in coarser fabric designs or applied occasionally in both woven or embroidered pieces to create textural effects.

Table mats, table cloths and tray cloths, curtains, and bags are obvious uses for the finer quality yarns.

14 Cotton

Cotton fibre
Cultivation

The cotton plant, although a perennial in its original tropical habitat, is almost entirely cultivated as an annual. Parts of India and Northern Brazil are the exceptions, where a tree-like bush thrives, growing a coarse type of brown or grey cotton. Cotton (*Gossypuim*) is of the mallow family, and there are many varieties of which the smallest may be no more than 1 ft (30 cm) high, and the largest up to 6 ft (1.8 m).

The flowering period is only about 12 hours. After pollination the *boll* (seed case) takes about 7 weeks to ripen, splitting open and revealing the *lint* which appears as a white fluffy ball, and must be picked immediately (figure 99). Some types also produce a short inferior fibre called lintoes, which is used in the manufacture of cotton wool, rayon, cellulose, etc. The lint fibre is hollow and cylindrical throughout growth.

99 The cotton plant

When the seed is mature and the boll bursts, the wall of the fibre collapses and the fibre itself twists in different directions (figures 101 and 102). A certain amount of wax is present in cotton fibres and is responsible for the degree of silkiness.

Fibre quality

Cotton qualities vary considerably. This is determined by length, uniformity and degree of whiteness. They are classed in the following order (though they are cultivated in many different countries besides).

Sea Island: 2 in (5 cm) staple (approx.)
Egyptian: $1\frac{3}{4}$ in (4.4 cm) staple

American – long stapled: $1\frac{1}{2}$ in (3.8 cm) staple
American – short stapled: 1 in (2.5 cm) staple
Indian and Chinese varieties: $\frac{3}{4}$ in (1.9 cm) staple

Harvesting

Harvesting, i.e. picking, is done either by hand, or with a mechanical picker, the locks being skilfully removed from the boll, and bagged. *Ginning* (the deseeding process) follows, the locks being fed through a cotton gin. In the industry the bales arrive at the mill and are graded and cleaned, the cotton is carded and converted to slivers prior to spinning.

100 The ripe cotton boll

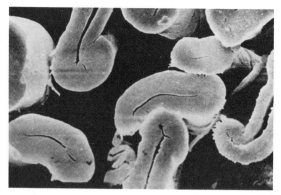

101 Cross section of cotton fibres under magnification

102 The walls of the cotton fibres collapse after picking

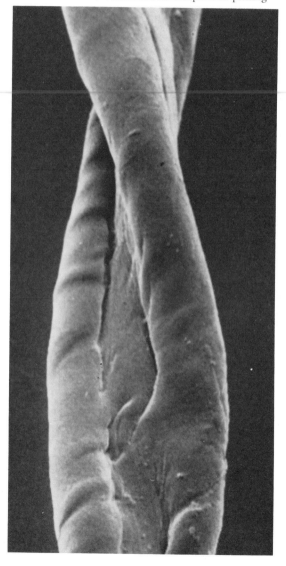

Preparation for spinning
Spinning equipment

Handspinning of cotton has been practised in many parts of the world for centuries, using a variety of spinning equipment, from small lightweight spindles with a slender tapered shaft to many types of wheels according to the area and the custom. For example, a spinning wheel was developed from an old bicycle wheel and simple wood frame, and used locally in cotton growing countries in Africa. Mahatma Gandhi introduced a light, compact and portable spinning wheel for general use throughout India to encourage people to spin at odd moments anywhere and at any time, and thereby improve the cotton cloth industry for the benefit of all (figure 103).

For the modern spinner in the West today a small supported spindle is simple, inexpensive and effective for the production of cotton yarn. Most well tuned wheels will also spin cotton well, and more quickly. A small orifice is adequate, as cotton should normally be spun fine.

Preparing the raw cotton

It is occasionally possible to obtain cotton in boll, in which case the hand spinner has the satisfaction (if added labour) of deseeding. It is a slow task, and quite hard on the hands. Raw cotton can also be obtained in the natural state after ginning but before the industrial removal of the tiny particles of seed by carbonisation. Hand spinning from cleaned and prepared rovings is not to be recommended in comparison with that of truly raw cotton, since the latter produces a far more characterful and attractive yarn.

The practice of *bowing* prior to carding is to be encouraged but not essential. The extreme fineness and shortness of the fibres hinders the effective separation of them. Bowing whips them apart into a light fluffy cloud, and carding them aligns them in an even film. Ideally carders mounted with extra-fine and close set card clothing is desirable. (A separate pair should be kept for cotton from that which is used for wool.)

3 Two forms of flax spinning; the flax on the left has been cross combed

4 Producing a thick yarn on an Indian Spinner – the drive band has been attached to the treadle of a sewing-machine table

5 Hand knitted shawl using 2 ply yarn spun from the natural coloured fleece of Soay, St Kilda, Shetland, Manx Loughton and Portland sheep.

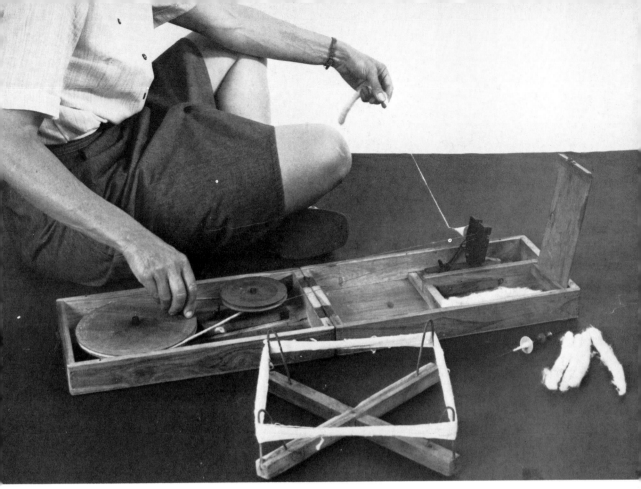

103 Portable modern Charka wheel

Bowing

1 Place a handful of raw cotton onto a smooth surface at waist height.

2 Put one end of the bow against the diaphragm, and the left arm along the bow grasping it firmly.

3 Hold it so that the catgut or cord lies along the top of the cotton and begin to pluck this cord with the right hand (figure 104). The cotton fibres will begin to fluff up as bowing proceeds. Some will adhere to the cord and these should be pulled off.

4 When the whole pile has attained a cloudy, whipped appearance, this should be put aside and another handful dealt with similarly. When sufficient cotton has been bowed, carding follows. Carding is not essential but facilitates spinning, and is needed if the long draw technique is used. Whipping can also be done with a wispy stick flaying into the pile of raw cotton, but it needs more skill for this to be done effectively.

Carding

Follow the instructions given for carding short wool (chapter 4, pages 33–37), spreading a small handful of whipped cotton across the width of the carder. Card as usual, *lightly* using brisk movements. Roll the carded fibres to produce a small, relatively dense rolag (figure 105).

Rolling can be done with the two hands towards the body, or on the back of the carder. It is also satisfactory to roll it sideways across the carder.

Spindle spinning

This can be done from a mass of bowed cotton or from a rolag. The small lightweight spindle is revolved either clockwise or anticlockwise and can be supported in a small shallow bowl or suspended, according to preference.

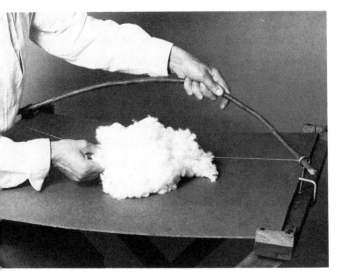

104 *Above* Bowing the raw cotton

105 Rolling a dense cotton rolag

106 *Below* Spindle spinning cotton from a rolag, the spindle being supported in a bowl

Drafting can be short, as in a semi-worsted, or longer, as skill increases. A true long draw action is possible, if rolags are used (figure 106), but this is most suitably accomplished on a wheel and it will be found that cotton needs a surprising amount of twist.

1 Grasping a handful of prepared cotton in the left hand, rotate the spindle, and attach a few fibres to the existing yarn.

2 Draw upwards with the left hand, allowing a few fibres to 'pay out' continuously against the tension supplied by the spindle, and control it with the finger and thumb of the right hand.

3 Roll the yarn slightly in the right hand as drafting proceeds to encourage even drafting and a uniform thread.

4 Apply sufficient twist for a strong fine yarn, but avoid corkscrew kinks along any section.

5 Repeat the process until winding on becomes necessary, and continue in this manner. (This method is not illustrated.)

Wheel spinning
Short draw method

A similar process can be used as on the spindle using either hand to hold the mass of cotton on the rolag and making a short drafting action between the hands, repeated a number of times before allowing the resultant length to

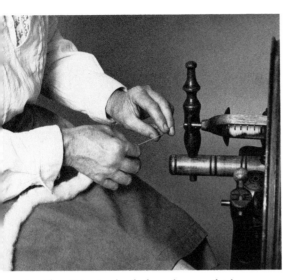

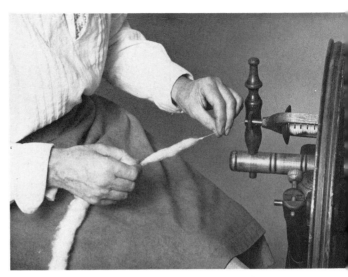

107 *Above* Spinning by the long draw method

109 *Below* Allowing the length to wind in quickly

108 Grasping the rolag in the right hand, with the left hand controlling the twist

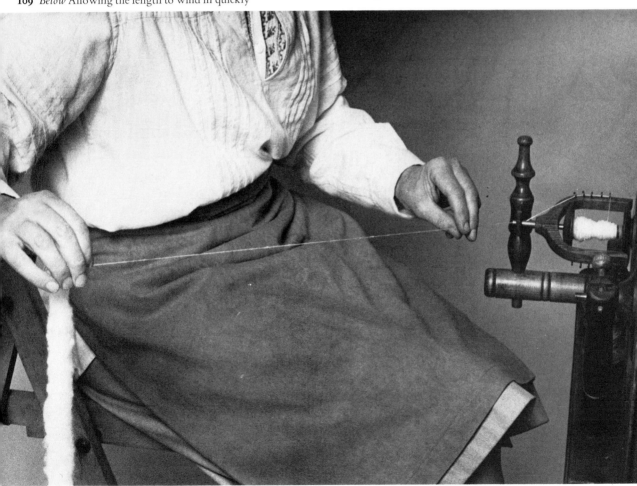

be fed onto the bobbin. Use a slack tension on the bands, and adjust as required.

Long draw method

The quicker and more satisfactory method of spinning cotton on a wheel is to adopt the long draw woollen spin using rolags. More twist is needed for cotton, however, to enable the short fibres to hold and to create a strong lively yarn. (Hand spun yarn is invariably more attractive as a singles yarn.)

1 After joining the rolag, rotate the wheel several times by a rapid treadling action, place the finger and thumb of the left hand on the yarn (figure 107), move the right hand about 2 in (5 cm) up the rolag and grasp it firmly (figure 108).

2 Draft carefully rolling the yarn held in the left hand in a slight untwisting movement at the same time (if needed).

3 Allow more twist to run through the left hand.

4 Employ short tugging movements with the right hand to cause the thicker areas along the yarn to thin out, whilst continuing to treadle (figure 109). Use a rolling action when necessary.

5 Aim for a fine, even yarn, and when sufficient twist is present allow the length to wind in very quickly.

Spinning from a roving

If the cotton is in roving form it may be necessary to divide it into slimmer portions. Using the left hand to control the twist, draft continuously to arm's length, with the right hand maintaining a short V-shaped flow of fibres. These are 'sucked' out of the roving by the combination of tension and twist.

Finishing processes
Washing

This is often not necessary until the yarn is woven. However, if discoloured, it is best soaked for an hour or more, boiled in good quality soap powder for about half an hour, then well rinsed in several baths of very hot soft water. The skeins should be shaken gently and dried at a slight tension.

Bleaching

This is not often required though the creamy colour habitually found in prepared rovings (through the processing) may be undesirable. The natural whiteness of the raw cotton can be restored by steeping in a bleaching bath (as for linen) for an hour or two, moving the skeins with a glass or wooden rod now and again. Care must be taken not to use too strong a solution. Rinse very thoroughly in soft warm water and hang, slightly weighted, to dry. Bleached cotton has a better affinity for dyeing than unbleached cotton.

Dyeing

Being pure cellulose, cotton has a good affinity for Direct Dyes, and these are suitable for use in small quantities in the home. Cotton also has an especial affinity for certain natural dyestuffs such as Kutch. Most other natural dyes, as used for wool and silk, will yield much paler shades on cotton.

Suggested uses for cotton yarn

A durable fibre in normal conditions, cotton has a number of valuable characteristics. The amount of twist in the composite yarns of a woven fabric will have much bearing on the character. For example, a high degree of twist and opposing direction of twist in alternate warp and weft threads will result in a crinkly effect after the cloth is off the loom. Conversely, a light twist will give a limp handle and a slightly fluffy surface.

Being absorbent, it is pleasant to wear in hot weather. Hand spun cotton fabrics normally have relatively thick thread and less ends and picks (threads) per inch than a commercial counterpart, resulting in less tendency to creasing. Shirts, tunics and ethnic garments of all kinds look well in hand spun cotton, particularly if restrained stripes or inlays are introduced. Smaller articles can include table mats, cushions and bags. It can also be used for crocheting and lace if well twisted and set.

15 *Other vegetable fibres*

Ramie, hemp, jute and nettle, like linen, are bast fibres, i.e. the fibre comes from the stem of the plant, and they can be hand spun to good effect for the right purposes. Sisal is a leaf fibre, while coir is taken from the fibrous husk of the coconut.

Ramie

This most resembles linen in quality. It is, however, white and extremely lustrous, and in sliver form looks surprisingly silk-like. It is exceptionally strong and is sometimes used industrially in place of linen. Not easily available in an unprepared state, it is usually obtainable in rovings. The fibres are considerably shorter than those of line, and in roving form can be spun direct, using a V-shaped drafting action, moving the right hand, which holds the roving, gradually out to arm's length and then letting it feed in quickly. The left hand controls the twist. Overspinning must be avoided. More tension is needed on the bands of the wheel than with cotton spinning.

Ramie has a beautiful handle if skilfully spun, and combines well with other fibres. Its natural lustre and softness offers possibilities for use with silk or mohair yarns, or even by blending on carders and rolling the fibres sideways into locks to be subsequently spun in a semi-worsted fashion.

Hemp

Hemp's original habitat was Central Asia, and it is almost as ancient a textile fibre as linen. It began to be cultivated in Asia Minor and parts of Europe about 1500 BC and is now widely grown, including in the United States of America. The harvesting and processing of the fibres for spinning is similar to that of flax, namely retting, breaking, scutching and hackling. It is longer and coarser, and has a higher level of tensile strength than most other natural fibres. It is suitable for furnishing fabrics and also for wearing apparel if suitably designed. Industrially it is also used for ropes, twines and much else.

Preparation and spinning should follow the same lines as that of linen. It is much coarser, and oil is sometimes used rather than water to assist the production of a smoother yarn.

Jute

Originating in India during the Neolithic age, jute was and still is extensively cultivated there and in Pakistan, as well as in certain parts of Brazil, the United States and Japan; many related species are more widely distributed. The plant is extremely tall, and as with other bast fibres, retting is an essential process in releasing the fibres.

Spinning should be done as with linen, but if received in roving or sliver form this may be easier if divided into short lengths, folded over the forefinger, and spun by drawing a few fibres forward with the left hand in long movements and feeding into the spindle at speed to prevent overtwisting.

Nettle

The common stinging nettle used to be harvested and prepared in much the same manner as flax, and the yarn woven into sheets and other 'linen' cloth as a substitute for line flax. There is a revival of this craft by individuals wishing to adopt traditional country customs and skills.

Sisal

This is a leaf fibre and not much used for hand spinning. It is considerably thicker and more

wiry than hemp, but has an attractive sheen
and a variety of shades from pale cream to a
brownish orange. It requires to be spun comparatively thick and having a long staple,
approximately 12 to 15 in (30 to 40 cm), is
rather difficult to handle. It is probably best to
use a distaff and prepare and dress it as for
linen.

Coir

The fibrous husk enveloping the hard shell of
the coconut kernel (a fruit fibre) is cultivated
in South India, Ceylon and Malaya. It is harvested, retted, winnowed and aligned. When
hand spun in those parts, the prepared fibre
mass is laid in front of the spinner and weighted with a stone. Spinning is done dexterously
between the fingers and coiled into the lap.
The modern hand spinner would not find the
spinning of coir very easy, and its use is
limited.

Part 4
The development of spinning techniques

The principles that yield beauty in crafts are unchanging and timeless . . . we must take a fresh look at real folkcraft of the past, for it is there that we may find healthy and genuine beauty expressed.

From *The Unknown Craftsman* by Soetsu Yanagi

16 The evolution of spinning

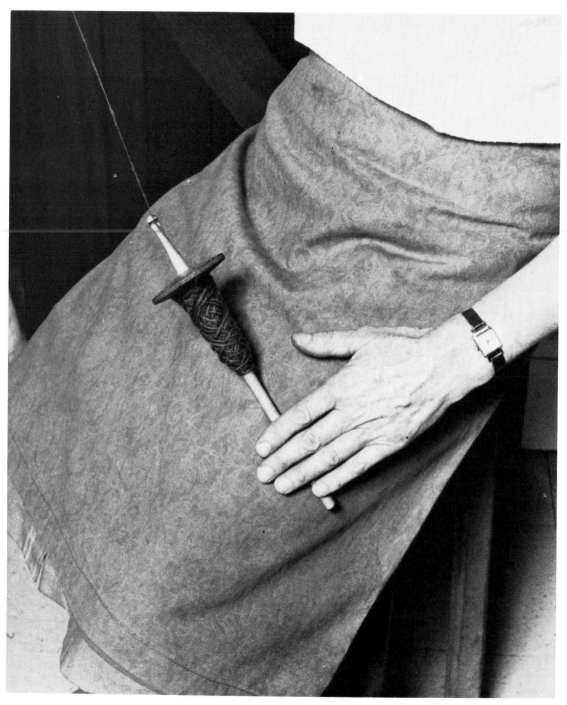

The evolution of spinning is of considerable interest to all serious spinning students. Its history is a long one dating back to Neolithic times or even earlier. Depending on the natural resources available to the early civilizations existing in various areas of the world, this skill naturally evolved in different ways. We do not know when the first wheel-driven spindle came to be invented, but it can be surmised that such tools were in use in the Far East during the Chinese Dynasty of Han, i.e. as far back as 2000 BC. Prior to this a hand operated spindle must have been used.

The spindle

In the Orient most of the spinning was probably that of cotton, silk, goat hair and some types of wool. These, together with China grass (Ramie), have been spindle spun throughout many centuries. Small supported spindles were adopted where very fine fibres were to be spun, and a few rare examples of silk fabrics of incomparable fineness still exist, and are proof of the almost unbelievable skill and dexterity of the spinners.

Almost equally beautiful were the Egyptian Mummy Cloths found in the ancient tombs, which were spindle spun and then woven on the simplest of looms; they date from about 5000 BC. These were exclusively of linen, usually undyed, supple and beautiful to handle, often composed of no less than 150 threads to the inch. Very careful preparation from harvesting onwards was practised, and due to the elevated position accorded the textile arts in the Egyptian and Mesopotamian civilizations at their zenith, much has been recorded (by pictorial paintings on walls of tombs and by decorative panels on vases) to furnish us with lasting evidence of their outstanding skills as spinners. One such illustration is to be seen depicting a woman using two spindles at once and spinning different qualities of linen on each!

It can be assumed that the very earliest method of spinning may have been a drafting and

110 Rolling a hip spindle down the thigh

twisting movement of fibres between the two hands, one hand simply inserting a few dexterous turns, and then winding the resulting lengths of yarn into a coil on the ground or onto a stick. An extension of this would naturally follow, namely to roll it along the thigh with the flat of the hand whilst drafting with the other. We know that the Greeks used this method, often employing a decorative 'sleeve' of smooth metal or leather on the thigh to facilitate rolling and to protect the garment of the spinner from staining.

The next logical development would be to roll the *spindle* along the thigh. The spindle might have a small metal hook or nick on the end, to guide the yarn. With the addition of a small weight (whorl) near the hook end, to increase impetus, it could be rolled on the thigh, and then allowed to fall free to continue spinning in mid air (figures 110 and 111). This type is found in the burial chambers of the Bronze Age people in Denmark, and has been widely used by primitive peoples in parts of Africa; it is also used amongst the Lapps, and in several South American countries. The raw fibres used would have varied a great deal in the different areas of the world.

The majority of weighted spindles have the whorl at the bottom. Some have been carved from one piece of wood and tapered into the spindle shaft. Others have had a flattish circular stone, or ring of baked clay, or even two curved pieces of wood or horn crossed at right angles and the spindle shaft inserted through a hole in the centre of each. By winding the yarn round the shaft over and under these slightly curved projections, a complete ball of yarn could be removed intact from the spindle by first drawing out the spindle and then the wooden pieces (see figure 2). In the Middle East it was not uncommon to find the women squatting on a low wall or stool and with bare feet rotating the lower part of the spindle by a brisk rub between the big toes, leaving both hands free for continuous drafting and winding.

People who are accustomed to squat on the ground not unnaturally tend to have their fibre

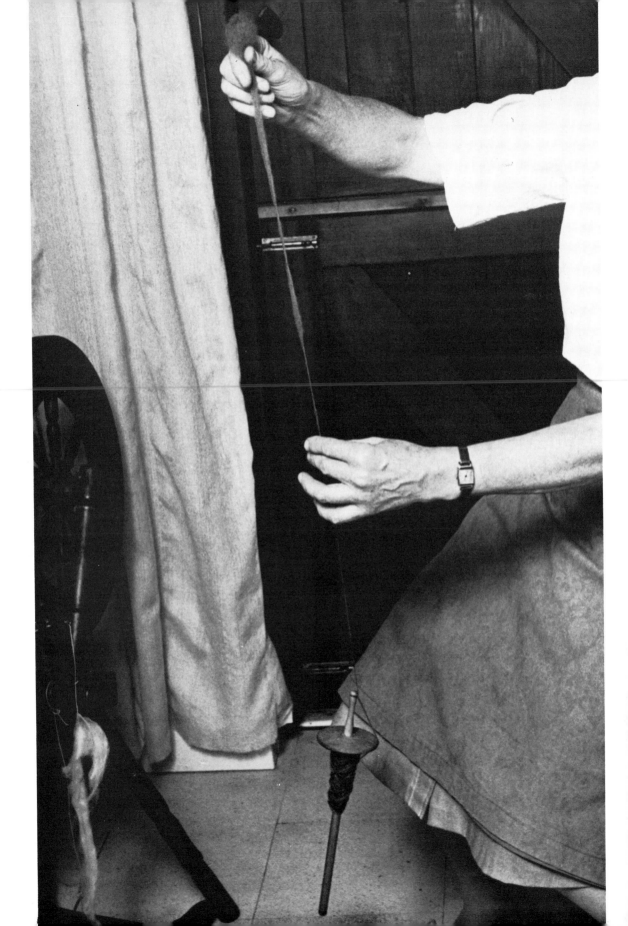

mass in front of them, and spinning is done by a rapid twisting of the spindle in the palm of the hand, held at arm's length and slightly above shoulder level. This method is still practised in the Sudan. (Ling Roth refers to it as the 'grasped' spindle.)

Perhaps the lightly weighted, slender shafted spindle used for cotton spinning in widely dispersed countries is of particular interest. It was usually supported in a bowl, a fine shallow basket, a gourd, or on the ground. In Guatemala, for instance, hand spun cotton is still spun in this way to the present day, the women usually squatting on the ground gossiping as they work. In the hotter climatic areas the spinner frequently rubs her hand over a lump of chalk to keep it dry.

The suspended spindle allows for more mobility on the part of the spinner, so often vital

to the execution of essential daily tasks, as for instance, when travelling by donkey or camel to new grazing grounds (e.g. the nomadic tribes of the Caucasus), the tending of the flocks or herds of goats, (e.g. Tibetan herdsmen, being also one example among many of men and boys spinning); and in the European countries especially, spindle spinning continued whilst stirring the dye pot or stew pot, rocking the cradle or travelling to market. Usually, for this purpose, the prepared fibres had to be drawn out into a sliver, or spun into rolags, and wound round and round the top of a long stick, the butt end of which was then tucked under the arm or in the belt. This stick is known as the distaff.

A more elaborate distaff made from a flat upright board fixed at right angles to a second board and often elaborately carved or ornately decorated in colour has been used in combination with a 'drop' (i.e. suspended) spindle in Russia and neighbouring countries around the

III *Left* Allowing the hip spindle to swing free

II2 *Below* Spindle spinning continues to be practised by the older women in Mediterranean countries

II3 The distaff is tucked under the arm

Baltic, for centuries. The spinner, having dressed the upright board with flax would place it along a bench, sit 'side saddle' on the horizontal part of the distaff, and with the left hand would spin the spindle drafting the fibres between the distaff and spindle. The whorls of these spindles were usually ball shaped and often gaily painted. Similar small spherical whorls on long thin shafts colourfully decorated are also to be found in use for cotton spinning, principally in certain African states to this day.

It is in Greece, Italy and some Balkan states that spindle spinning from a balcony was not uncommon practice in recent centuries. It enabled the spinner to create a tremendous length of yarn between each winding on stage. She inserted an extra large amount of twist in the short length, then at the same time as she moved her hand a generous distance up the rolag she cast the spindle over the balcony rail. Twist rushed up into the fibres as the impetus and weight caused rapid extensive drafting. The spindle naturally retained the forward twisting motion longer than is usual on the normal draft and the yarn received sufficient twist from the initial spin. With dexterous movements the yarn was wound in a figure-of-eight onto the finger and thumb before the spindle began to reverse, and was subsequently wound onto the base of the spindle. The whole process was repeated ad infinitum.

In passing it is interesting to note that there are a number of 'Spinning Galleries' in old farmsteads in the English Lake District. Though built in the spinning wheel period, i.e. mostly during the latter half of the seventeenth and early eighteenth centuries, it could be a matter for conjecture that these balconies may also have been used in this same way. The wool in those parts would have been carded for woollen spinning. The name 'Spinning Galleries' may be misleading, for the principal purpose of them appears to be as a sorting and storage agea for the fleece and possibly for hanging the spun skeins to dry. There seems

114 Using a distaff and spindle allows mobility

little doubt, however, that as groups of neighbouring spinners were wont to congregate with their wheels and knitting on winter evenings around a fire, they would also sit in the galleries at work on summer days.

It is not possible to determine when spindle spinning gave way to that of the wheel. It was a gradual process, taking place at different periods in different areas of the world. At the present day there are peoples who have never ceased to use the spindle since prehistoric times and may still continue to do so for centuries to come. Suffice to say that the transition has occurred in the main during a span of several centuries according to the needs, life style and particular cultural developments of each race. Migrations of people, trading, conquests, population increases, religious persecutions, explorations and inventions were all factors which brought about changes and pressures for greater production and speedier output. Mere survival dictated a need for resourcefulness, though often offset by a natural disinclination towards change.

The spinning wheel
Spindle wheel

As a direct evolutionary development from the drop spindle the spindle wheel, as its name suggests, is a wheel designed to rotate the spindle. Turned on its side and supported on an upright by leather loops, horn bearings or other devices, the spindle can be turned at high speed if a groove is made on the circumference of the whorl, and a cord at tension, taken round both this and a large wheel. The wheel is also mounted on an upright fixed to the same base. It is a very simple and effective tool, having especially accurate control of yarn quality in the hands of a skilled spinner.

This spindle wheel played a very important part in the evolutionary development of spinning in Europe, and was in use over a span of several centuries alongside the more complicated flyer wheel. It is said to have derived from India and it is generally accepted that spindle wheels of various constructions were in use in the Middle and Far East from the ninth or tenth centuries onwards. Most of these early wheels were mounted on a low base, and the spinner, squatting on the ground beside it, turned the wheel with the right hand and spun with the left. Many and varied are the developments of these wheels particularly those in China where the spinning of wild silk, cotton and ramie must have required the highest degree of skill. Exquisitely fine and extraordinarily beautiful fabrics from these periods show indisputable proof of this. Many of these wheels were constructionally comparatively light, often having bamboo spokes, two rim edges, and a criss-cross lashing in place of a solid rim.

Somewhat similar wheels came to be in use in Turkey, Greece and neighbouring countries, though many of these were mounted on short legs, thus raising both wheel and spindle to a

height more conveniently operated from either a standing or sitting position.

Developments of these early wheels show attachments of a handle or use of a finger stick, whilst in other instances there are ingenious methods for freeing the right hand by attaching a long foot treadle to the spokes, and mounting a second spindle for use of the freed right hand.

Spindle wheels having this type of light framework and criss-cross lashings of cord, gut or strips of leather to take the driving band were simple and inexpensive to make and came to be used to a limited extent in many parts of Europe (figure 115).

The solid wood rimmed wheel, however, is the more generally recognised tool in the Western world. Both this and the rimless type were originally mainly used for cotton and other short stapled fibres including shortwools, and after the invention of the flyer

115 A Greek spindle wheel with a criss-cross lashed rim

wheel the spindle wheel came to be known as the short fibre wheel, while the flyer wheel was called the long fibre wheel (for flax and longwools etc.). A similar wheel has also been generally used throughout the centuries for the winding of spools and bobbins.

In Britain a number of shapes, styles and wheel-to-spindle ratios have evolved according to individual ideas and requirements, but almost all have had solid rims. Occasionally these have been shaped in sections from solid pieces of wood making a very large heavy wheel capable of prolonged rotation after the spinner has ceased to drive the wheel with her hand. The majority however have a hooped rim composed of two lengths of approximately $\frac{1}{4} \times 3\frac{1}{2}$ in (6 × 90 mm) pliable wood such as chestnut, which after thorough soaking in running water can be bent round a template and laced or riveted into place and attached to the spoke ends. They are known variously as Great wheel (figure 116) (a fairly general term and used widely in England), and Long wheel, particularly in Ireland, where it has continued in use in isolated spots until the middle of this century. The Muckle wheel is the Scottish term. In Wales it is not unnaturally referred to as the Welsh wheel, and it continued to be used exclusively through the centuries following the advent of the Saxony or flyer wheel, (long stapled fibres being virtually unknown to the Welsh). The original introduction of the Great wheel to Britain was probably through the Dutch and Flemish textile workers who brought many of their skills to England in the Medieval period. Though it is difficult to imagine that there had been no advancement from the simple drop spindle by a few resourceful individuals here and there prior to this, no records have come to light to prove this.

To a lesser extent than the revival of the Saxony flyer type, this Great wheel (High wheel, Walking wheel are yet further names) has come to be used by specialist spinners today. There are many models in use, each depending on the features they are designed to emulate in the earlier wheels. For example

various forms of tensioning devices are used, possibly the most primitive being the length of plaited straw looped round the spindle shaft and threaded through two holes bored in the upright. This bearing of plaited 'rope' could be drawn tighter as required.

The length and thickness of the spindle varies according to the quality (size) of yarn to be spun. The spindle mounting also varies considerably including the ratio of spindle whorl diameter and that of the wheel diameter. The higher the ratio, the greater the revolutions of the spindle to a single turn of the wheel. A slightly smaller circumference wheel (which may be less tiring to operate) is able to provide a high speed drive if a secondary pulley is mounted above the spindle, the single band from the wheel driving this pulley on the small diameter groove, while a short band is carried round this large pulley and on round the small diameter groove on the spindle shaft. This elaboration seems not to have been used in the Oriental and European types but was brought into fairly general use in North America in the nineteenth century.

Relatively few spindle wheels are designed for comfortable use in a seated position, though a few of the more solidly built wheels which have sufficient weight to continue to rotate on their own enable the spinner to use both hands for greater control when longer fibres are being spun. Occasionally ancient illustrations are to be seen of a handle attached to a spoke on the wheel, including a famous picture from a fourteenth-century illuminated manuscript.

Flyer wheel

An early development from the spindle wheel was that of the hand operated flyer wheel. An improvement in speed and continuous spinning was achieved by the addition of the U-shaped wooden or metal flyer to the spindle head, and the insertion of a removable bobbin. The spinner was usually seated and the wheel, being somewhat less in diameter than its forerunner, was often turned by a handle attached to a spoke or to the axle. Later a treadle attachment to the axle crank allowed

both hands to be free to form the yarn. The Saxony wheel, attributed to the German, Johann Jurgen, in 1530, is undoubtedly the forerunner of the treadle flyer wheels from that time onwards. Many of the modern flyer wheels in use today show little change of design from those used in Europe in the 'spinning wheel' period (figure 117).

It is generally known that Leonardo da Vinci drew out working plans for a spinning device in 1490 that was so far in advance of his time that it was never used. It was designed as a small neat appliance to be rotated by hand, but with the great advantage that the flyer moved back and forward along the spindle thereby building the cop along the bobbin, automatic-

116 *Left* A modern Great wheel

117 *Below* Three antique flyer wheels (from left to right): Irish flax wheel, Shetland upright wheel, Hebridean wheel

ally. Few wheels were subsequently designed to incorporate this device and in most cases it was the bobbin that travelled along the spindle shaft. These were probably intended for spinning fine linen (figures 118 and 119).

Spinning in India

There seems little doubt that the form of cotton spinning so extensively used throughout India has changed little since the first use of the wheel in the tenth or eleventh centuries. The Indian name is charka, and in certain areas at the present time groups of women can be seen working on this attractive low wheel. It has been generally superseded however by the small, compact and portable 'Gandhi' wheel (figure 103), evolved by him in 1920 in a partially successful attempt at encouraging the women of town and village to build up small home industries to supply the vital textile

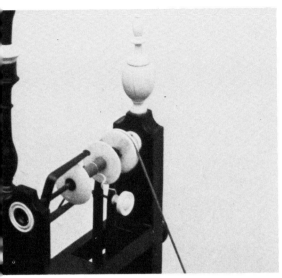

118 *Left* This mahogany flax wheel has an automatic movement of the bobbin along the spindle shaft to facilitate an even build up of yarn

119 *Above* Detail of the automatic spindle head

export industry with hand spun weft yarns, and also to clothe themselves.

Recent information sent by a native of Bombay describes the method of preparation of the cotton into rolags, as still used today. The cotton is bowed, and the string, which is 2 ft to 2½ ft (60 to 75 cm) long, is rubbed over with wax to prevent the cotton fibres from sticking to it. A flat wooden plate is used for deseeding. After cleaning and carding, the film of fibres is spread onto a wooden plate. A small stick is held in one hand, whilst the other rolls the cotton around the stick. A presser is then used to press it firmly round the stick and this latter is then gently extracted. The resultant rolag is a tiny dense pencil-like sliver. Hand woven cloth from this hand spun yarn is known as pure Khadi.

The method of spinning is similar to that used on the Great wheel. The spinner, in this case, sits on the ground on the projecting bar thereby holding the mechanism steady and rotates the wheel with the right hand whilst the left hand drafts the sliver at a 45° angle. Though the wheel is small, it has a gear system which speeds up the revolutions of the spindle, and as cotton needs a relatively large number of turns per inch for adequate strength, this is effectively achieved on this neatly made little instrument. A hand driven wheel has been produced in recent years which holds several spindles.

Mechanised spinning wheels

The history of making yarn has, therefore, evolved through a series of gradual developments from the simple hand spindle to the wheel-driven spindle, and thence to the flyer wheel. Then, with the Industrial Revolution in Britain, came the multiple spindle wheel (the Spinning Jenny), followed by Samuel Crompton's semi-mechanised Mule in 1770 and Arkwright's Water Frame, and eventually the Ring Spinner and Cap Spinner, which, with a modern development of the Mule, are in general use in the natural fibre mills today.

The Spinning Jenny was invented by James Hargreaves in 1764 (figure 120). Several replicas of the Spinning Jenny have been made (figure 121) and used in recent years and it is not impossible to imagine that the technically-minded spinning enthusiasts may be tempted to re-introduce it into their homes today! It is designed for a woollen spin with a hand controlled drafting system operated with one hand, which drafts and winds on to eight or more spindles concurrently. Special carding preparation is required and considerable skill in the overall operation. However the ability to produce a number of yarns in a single operation may appeal to the few, and would form a link with their ancestors of the immediate pre-Industrial Revolution era.

Felt making

A word should be said in passing with regard to the ancient art of felt making, as in many cases this initially entails the preparation and spinning of the fibres. It has been used in many forms through history to the present day, and the modern hand spinner could find a place for this process in order to achieve certain desirable effects.

Wonderful examples of heavily felted woven

120 A reconstruction of the original model of Hargreaves' Spinning Jenny (Photograph: Crown Copyright, Science Museum, London)

and knitted caps dating from the early Bronze Age are to be seen in the National Museum in Copenhagen, Denmark, and are from the burial grounds in Jutland of about 3500 years ago.

In Tudor times in Britain, knitted caps often underwent a heavy felting process, rendering them both firm and enduring. Both woven and knitted fabrics and garments were pounded and shrunk to a degree that made them resistant to sword and spear. The Chinese used felt shields and armour and even made felt boats. Nomadic peoples in Turkistan and neighbouring countries built their tents of felt which lasted a lifetime and afforded protection against all weathers, but in this case there was no prior spinning and weaving or knitting processes involved. These kinds of felts are produced by the laying of film upon film of fibres and pounding them with a soap solution until they hold firmly together in a thick stiff blanket, sometimes arranged in colours to

121 A later replica of the Spinning Jenny (Photograph: Crown Copyright, Science Museum, London)

produce an elaborate surface design. The horse blankets of the Turkomen of Iran are a fine example of the art. Careful preparation of the fleece is required, using a special combing process, and the fleece may also be dyed where coloured patterns are to be introduced.

17 Spinning on the Great wheel

Revival of the technique

A detailed study of the method of spinning on the Great wheel is included here, since many of these wheels have been rescued from attics and cellars in recent years, and copies are being made for use by serious students of spinning. It is therefore appropriate to consider the mode of spinning as developed from these early wheels.

The revival of the spindle wheel stems from the desire of many aspiring spinners to follow the earlier skills of their forbears to their ultimate. Side by side with a tendency to create rough and random textured yarns today, there runs an instinctive longing to recreate the excellence of craftsmanship, in all its facets within the bounds of the spinner's skill, and which was a natural trait of our ancestors throughout several centuries. It is generally known that the Great wheel was more suited to the production of the perfect yarn for the shortwool types and the woollen spin, as great control can be achieved when the turn is effected by hand, as the twisting process ceases immediately the wheel is stopped. Moreover no further twist is inserted in the winding-on stage.

An exceptionally fine worsted yarn can also be spun on this wheel. The fibre quality must be in the high count range, e.g. 70s to 80s or more (fine Merino) and not too long in the staple. If the fibres are well combed and a number of locks held in a bunch in the left hand, these can be paid out in a true worsted alignment. Plying on the spindle wheel can be done satisfactorily but is not quite so easy to control if the yarn has a high degree of twist present. It is normally preferable to turn the wheel in a clockwise direction. Should the direction of twist need to be reversed, as is the case when plying, this presents little problem if the wheel band is crossed between the spindle and whorl in a figure-of-eight, and the wheel driven clockwise as usual. The spindle will then rotate anticlockwise. The yarns to be plied need to be tensioned to prevent snarling.

With a freshly opened lock of a newly sheared fleece of quality it is with the utmost ease and pure joy that one spins a uniform and continuous thread on a well tuned Great wheel. Well made, in good repair, its bearings frequently oiled, this tool allows for more variety of rhythmic movement and consequently a higher degree of pleasure in its use than that of the flyer wheel. Its drawback is largely that the spinner needs to work standing, or even walking backwards and forwards if the wheel is sufficiently heavy to keep rotating by its own impetus. This naturally needs more space (hence the occasional name of Walking wheel).

Woollen spin

It must first be realised that twist is inserted from near the tip of the spindle each time the yarn coiled along it drops off the point as the spindle rotates.

1 Attach a 2 ft (60 cm) length of hand spun yarn to the spindle shaft near to the whorl. A sleeve of brown paper can be rolled round the area which is to receive the completed thread if so desired. This spool, when filled, can then be drawn off the spindle intact. Turn the wheel just enough to wind this yarn diagonally to the tip of the spindle.

2 Using a rolag, cradle it in the left hand. Hold the end of the yarn from the spindle taut in the same hand between the second and third finger and underneath the rolag, with the palm of the hand facing downwards (figure 122). Bring the angle from the spindle tip to the hand to about 45°.

122 Splicing the join on the spindle

3 Now begin to turn the wheel with the right hand by pressing on one spoke. Allow a few fibres from the rolag end to adhere to the twisting yarn, overlapping about 4 in (10 cm), and drafting slightly as soon as the join is complete.

4 Back off (i.e. reverse the wheel just enough to remove the spiralling thread from the tip end of the spindle), and move the left hand (which is holding the yarn at the rolag juncture) across the body until the yarn is parallel with the wheel band.

5 Rotate the wheel again slowly in a clockwise direction in order to wind the yarn onto the spindle near the whorl end. It is necessary to retain sufficient length to spiral back along to the spindle tip and still have a length of about 12 in (30 cm) from that point to the rolag junction.

6 Maintain a firm hold at this point, returning to the 45° position, and rotate the wheel several times.

7 Allow the left hand to move about 2 in (5 cm) up the rolag without disturbing its shape. Grip it firmly in this position and immediately draw backwards whilst continuing to rotate the wheel at a uniform speed.

8 When drafting and twist are complete, back off, align the thread as described in stage 4, and wind on. The yarn should be wound on evenly with a gradual tapering at either end, and occupy no more than half the spindle shaft.

Technical considerations

To master this skill to perfection the following technical points should be understood.

1 Wheel-to-spindle-whorl ratio determines the number of twists per inch along the thread in a single turn of the wheel. If a wheel diameter is, say 50 in (125 cm), and the whorl groove is 1 in (2.5 cm), the ratio is termed 50:1.

2 A consistently maintained relation between the length of each draft to the number of revolutions of the wheel results in the overall uniformity of the yarn. Rolags must also be as uniform as possible in all respects. Drafting is best kept to a convenient arm's length, and this is economical in time, and less tiring than an extended length necessitating moving away from the rotating wheel. Moreover it is easier to keep a count of the number of turns of the wheel if the right hand turns it continuously. (If counting presents a problem a simple device can be fixed to flick over a protrusion on one spoke, and the sound produced indicates one revolution.)

3 Twist begins to be inserted into the yarn on about the last 1 in (2.5 cm) of the spindle as it drops off the tip.

4 No further twist is applied to the yarn after the wheel is reversed and the yarn is being wound onto the cop. This is not the case with the flyer wheel.

Correctives

Both hands can, on occasion, be used to correct an unwanted slub, using a backwards rolling action between the finger and thumb of the right hand (on the spindle side of the slub) and allowing a further drafting by the left hand.

If the yarn has received excessive spin, the wheel may need to be reversed and the left hand moved forward along the yarn and further drafting effected. Or, conversely, the wheel can be stopped, the left hand can be moved further up the rolag to allow excess twist to run up into the new section of the rolag, and then the yarn can be drafted again.

Worsted type spin

The worsted type spin is not traditionally practised on the Great wheel, but it can easily be accomplished (1) using wool combed tops, or (2) direct from the fleece.

Spinning from combed tops

A relatively short and fine stapled fleece is needed as the drafting has to be done with the left hand only (a Longwool would cause

123 *Above* Spinning with an alpaca mixture on the Great
wheel

124 *Below* Controlling the wheel with the right hand

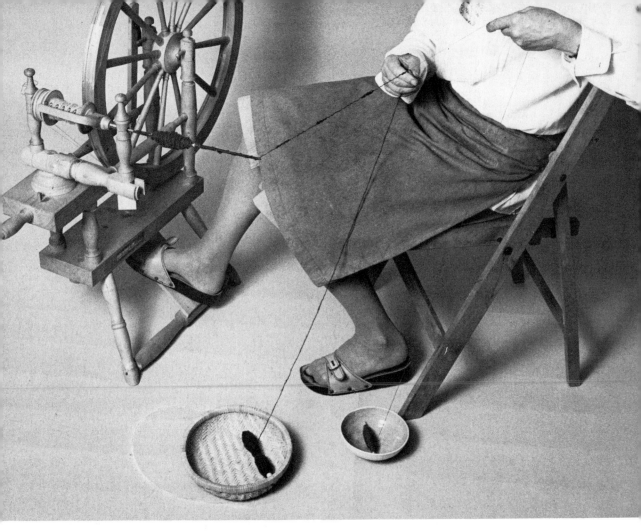

125 Creating a spiral knot yarn on an improvised spindle set into the orifice of a flyer wheel

126 *Right* Winding on

Spinning direct from the fleece

This means that the fleece should be prepared minimally but sufficiently to allow the locks to draft smoothly and freely in a similar manner to that of the combed tops. The fleece will work better if it is newly sheared, and if the tips and butt are eased open, if needed. Each lock is attached to the yarn from the butt (root) end, and drafted along the lower edge, allowing the fibres to pay out evenly. A medium staple and fairly open fleece is desirable for this method.

difficulties). Divide the top into short lengths of about 6 in (15 cm). Take one of these, hold it firmly in the left hand, and join by overlapping with the yarn attached to the spindle. Rotating the wheel, begin to draft, allowing a few overlapping fibres to be drawn out from the lower edge of the lock. Continue drafting to arm's length, back off and wind on. If strict control of the lock is maintained, total fibre alignment is preserved and a quality thread achieved.

A recent world record of the finest wool yarn to be spun, was that of a 100s quality Merino combed top, which was produced on a Great wheel at a ratio of 113 miles (180 km) to 1 lb (440 g) weight of yarn!

Plying

1 The cops, on their paper core, should be threaded onto the lowest rods of a spool rack

and laced in and out of a series of rods above it, in order to create slight tension.

2 The two ends are tied to a coil of paper (a large pirn) wound round the spindle shaft as described before. The spool rack is placed well behind and to the left of the spinner.

3 After inserting the forefinger between the two threads, hold them at an angle of 45° from the spindle tip, revolve the wheel in an anti-clockwise motion (or apply crossed bands and a clockwise motion). Observe the number of twists per inch in a given length, say 18 in (45 cm). If this is as required, back off and wind on.

4 Repeat stage 3 continuously, maintaining just sufficient tension forward of the left hand, and from the cops, to prevent snarling or uneven plying.

Correcting faults

1 If the drive band is 'thrown' either the wheel axle is slack or the wheel is warped. Drive band slippage indicates too slack a band. This must be removed and retied or spliced, or renewed if greasy.

2 If the spindle point 'circles' it is either bent or out of alignment and needs retuning.

3 If yarn breakage occurs when spinning, check the angle of yarn flow from the spindle tip. It should be at an angle of about 45°. Try also giving more turns of the wheel before drafting, or draft less quickly.

4 If the yarn is too thick, it probably lacks sufficient drafting. To correct this move the left hand further up the rolag and continue drafting without adding more turns of the spindle (i.e. stop the wheel whilst correcting this fault) and then continue spinning using a slightly quicker attenuation or slightly more rolag.

5 If the yarn is too thin, break off and rejoin using a good splicing join. To avoid spinning too thin a yarn, check that the rolags are rolled firmly enough to draft evenly and relate your speed of drafting to the revolutions on the wheel. The larger the wheel diameter the more turns the spindle makes per wheel revolution. Each turn of the spindle puts one twist into the yarn as it drops off the spindle tip.

Improvising a spindle wheel

An improvised spindle wheel can be made comparatively easily on a flyer wheel by fashioning a slim, tapered shaft and wedging it into the orifice of the flyer wheel so that it protrudes about 6 in (15 cm). A heavy gauge knitting needle can serve the purpose provided it fits firmly into the orifice and is in alignment with the spindle (figure 125). The footman is best unhitched and the wheel turned by hand (figure 126). This is one way of overcoming the problems of making a lumpy, textured yarn which resists passing through the orifice and hooks on a flyer mechanism.

Part 5
Equipment

*Let us give cheers for that age when again
many beautiful unsigned goods are produced . . .
and are used as a matter of course in daily life.*

From *The Unknown Craftsman* by Soetsu Yanagi

18 *Choice, construction and maintenance of equipment*

Spinning wheels
Buying a wheel

The economic factor is not normally one which can be ignored, and the most expensive wheel is not necessarily the most desirable buy. The increasing number of sources of supply make it both easier to obtain a wheel and more difficult to select wisely. Advice from an expert or really experienced spinner is a valuable asset where possible. Avoid buying too hurriedly; weigh the pros and cons of different types and makes. Never procure a wheel solely for its looks! If purchasing an antique wheel, or a second-hand wheel, investigate its working capabilities thoroughly. Do not necessarily turn it down if it appears not to work or has missing parts; these can often be rectified by oiling and tuning, or by the replacement of a faulty or absent component. There are occasions when a 'difficult' wheel needs nothing more than a new driving band (a fine high twist saddler's twine will often be the solution).

The wheel-to-spindle ratio should be understood as this has a bearing on the type of spinning achieved. It is this ratio which determines the number of twists per inch along the thread in a single turn of the wheel (e.g. if the wheel diameter is 20 in (50 cm) and the whorl groove of the spindle is 1 in (2.5 cm), the ratio is termed 20:1. A marked differential between the diameter of the spindle pulley groove and that of the bobbin groove is also an essential if over-twisting the yarn is to be prevented – the spindle pulley must be the greater. For general purposes and a fairly large output, too small a wheel should be avoided. A 24 in (60 cm) or 26 in (65 cm) wheel is desirable. Ensure that the treadling action is light and effortless. Avoid a very small orifice, unless the wheel is intended solely for linen, cotton, fine worsted and other high count yarns.

Note the type of bearings, as metal bearings are normally the most durable (and these are often made adjustable). Nylon can be satisfactory and is also very durable. Leather bearings on the maidens need to be thick, strong and firmly positioned in the uprights. If metal bearings are too tight, a little graphite grease or oil helps to ease them.

The wheel and the spindle shaft and whorl must be 'true' when in motion. A wheel wobble is liable to 'throw' the bands, whilst a pulley which is not set true on the spindle shaft may cause an uneven drag on the drive band. The tension adjustment requires to be very sensitive and the mother-of-all must be stable on the base (or saddle).

The driving wheel should be made of well seasoned hardwood. It should have a good smooth finish and a beeswax polish rather than a polyurethane surface. Varnish should be avoided. If a wheel is bought in kit form it should be well sanded before assembly, stained if desired, and wax polished thoroughly, using several applications. It can, if desired, be sealed with the application of a thin coating of matt polyurethane, any surplus of which is then wiped off. When dry, the wax polish can be applied and polished.

Some New Zealand wheels incorporate a light metal framework to support the spindle-flyer assembly, whilst all-metal wheels are to be found very occasionally. Improvised wheels are to be seen from time to time using a bicycle wheel but are not to be found as a marketable proposition!

An ever increasing number of spinning wheels are arriving on the market today, some of which are given highly descriptive names for identification. This can cause confusion as the name used by one craftsman does not necessarily relate directly to that of a similar model produced by another wheel maker. The important feature about each is that it is a good sound tool able to do what is required of it.

A wheel of whatever type, should be, (a) a suitable tool for the kind of spinning required, (b) in good lasting condition, and (c) a delight to use. Moreover if it is likely to be taken about by car on frequent occasions, it should not be too delicately balanced a wheel. A compact precision tool such as a well built upright wheel having a wheel diameter of approximately 17 in (43 cm) should stand up well both to travelling, and to use by a number of learner spinners, if required for this purpose.

Range of types available

Saxony wheel

The term Saxony wheel (see figure 33) is now loosely used to describe the horizontal wheel (as opposed to the vertical or upright wheel) and is the name given to the original long fibre, treadle driven, continuous action wheel evolved early in the sixteenth century. The variations were numerous and this holds good in today's models. Many well-made craftsman-built wheels are now on the market. The Norwegian type is a beautiful looking wheel and has many desirable features, including a large diameter driving wheel, and wheel alignment mechanism. It is often embellished with extra refinements, but is usually an expensive wheel to buy (see figure 3).

Lighter weight, smaller framed wheels are exported from New Zealand, and are crafts-man-made in Great Britain and other countries also. To compensate for the small diameter, the wheel itself is made with a thicker, deeper rim and, in some instances, a small lead weight or two is embedded in it to assist rotation.

Upright wheel

There are a number of upright wheel types, known also as vertical wheels, and sometimes loosely termed Castle wheels (though strictly speaking the latter name is confined to those having the wheel mounted above the flyer complex). A great variety of types are on the market or individually made. The small

Shetland wheel (see figure 3), is one which is emulated a great deal. An excellent precision tool is one exported from Norway (see figure 3). Most Scandinavian models are light in colour, being made from silver birch and are finished with a polyurethane sealer. An upright wheel can be equally as satisfactory as a Saxony, and it takes up less space. A small, firmly made wheel can travel in a car easily and without harm.

Single-band wheel with Scotch tensioner (Ashford wheel)

Most of the wheels being made today are based on one or other of the earlier models of the Spinning Wheel period in history. Many are more or less precise replicas, though very few of these employ the friction drag (Scotch tensioner). There are, however, an increasing number being made which are a modification of or departure from the traditional wheels. The long established and undeniably popular Ashford wheel from New Zealand is an example of this. It is generally acclaimed as the best value as it is soundly constructed of seasoned beech and its orifice and flyer hooks are sufficiently large to allow the thicker slubby yarns to be spun without trouble. The combined Scotch tensioner and tension screw, moreover, allow for fine adjustment. Its main asset is its relatively low price. These wheels are mass produced and have a worldwide market. They can be obtained in kit form or assembled from a number of agents in Great Britain, America and elsewhere.

Indian spinner

An Indian spinner, mounted on a treadle sewing machine frame or other purpose built base, is strongly recommended for thick bulky yarns for rug wefts, as it has an extra large orifice and bobbin (see figure 59).

Jumbo flyer

The Jumbo flyer assembly designed for use on an Ashford wheel is also invaluable for bulky yarns (see figure 60).

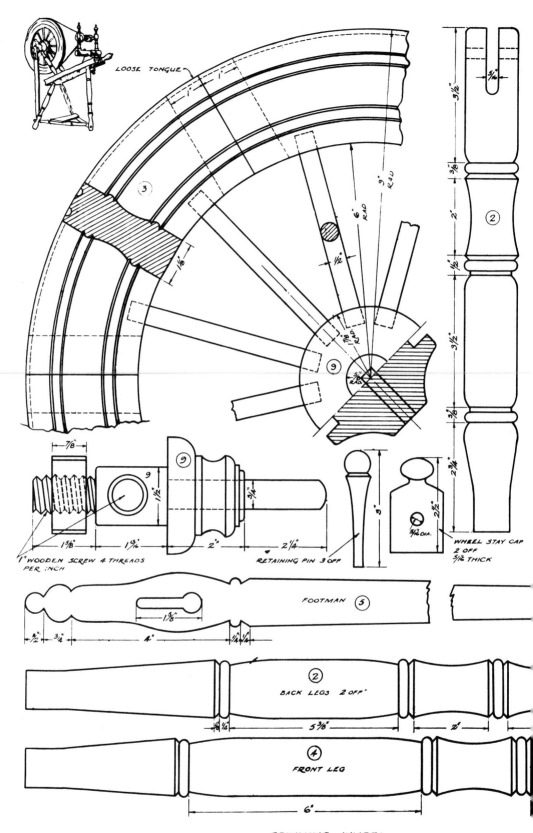

LOOSE TONGUE

③

⑨

6" RAD

3" RAD

½"

⅛"

⁷⁄₁₆ RAD

⁵⁄₁₆ RAD

⑨

⁵⁄₁₆"

3½"

³⁄₈"

2"

½"

3½"

③⁄₈"

2¾"

②

⑦⁄₈"

9

1½"

¾"

9

2"

2¼"

1⅝"   1⁹⁄₁₆"

1" WOODEN SCREW 4 THREADS
PER INCH

RETAINING PIN 3 OFF

3"

2½"

³⁄₁₆ DIA.

WHEEL STAY CAP
2 OFF
³⁄₁₆ THICK

FOOTMAN ⑤

⁵⁄₈"
1⅛"

½"   ¾"   4"   1¼" ½"

② BACK LEGS 2 OFF

⅛" ¼"   5³⁄₈"   2"

④ FRONT LEG

6'

SPINNING WHEEL
REPRODUCED BY RURAL INDUSTRIES BUREAU BY PERMISSION OF
THE DESIGNER P AINSLIE

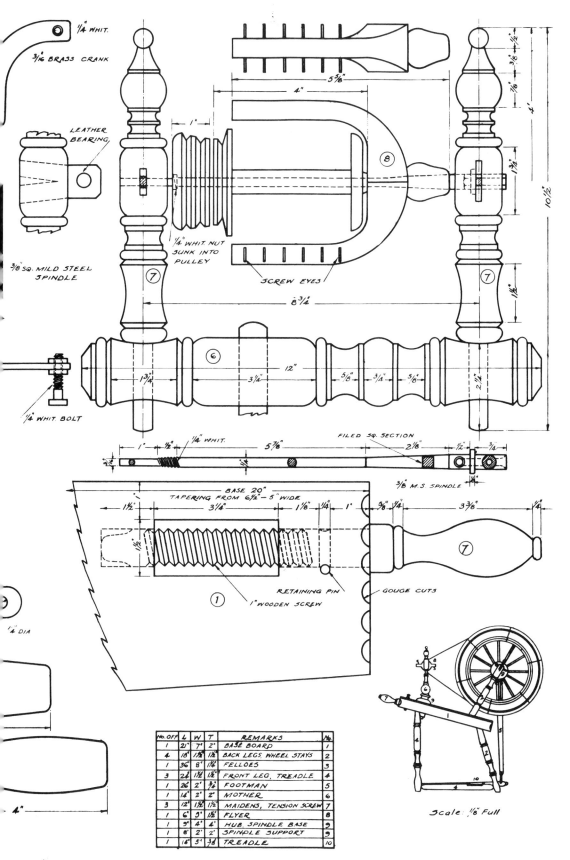

127 A blueprint for making a flyer spinning wheel

Great wheel

A Great wheel also has its place in the context of producing thick and effect yarns, and besides being a lovely tool to use, it has its own simplicity and beauty (see figure 116).

Constructing a wheel

Spinning wheels are available in kit form from many suppliers. The building of a spinning wheel from scratch is a skilled operation requiring a great deal of expertise, but for the experienced woodturner a blueprint of a spinning wheel designed by P. Ainslie is reproduced here for interest (figure 127).

Maintenance

A spinning wheel is both a working tool and a piece of furniture and should be treated with the respect and care due to it in both roles. It is a simple piece of machinery, but finely tuned, having bearings and joints that need frequent lubrication.

To preserve the main part of it, the wood, it should initially be treated with a good wood sealer and/or beeswax, and given subsequent applications from time to time. This is dependent on the amount of use and the conditions in which it is kept, including temperature and humidity changes. If it is used for fleece spun in the grease, it may be necessary to wipe it over with a rag soaked in paraffin or turpentine (denatured alcohol) occasionally, followed by a good beeswax polish. A matt polyurethane sealing process (rubbed in with a cloth, and the excess rubbed off immediately) is a good base for the polish and preserves the wood. Cedar oil is also beneficial to the wood but causes a reddish colouring.

Avoid standing a wheel too near a hot radiator or in direct sunlight. If the wheel warps or any part develops a crack, consult an expert spinning wheel builder.

Lubricate all metal bearings with a lightweight oil each time before use. If stiffness is present on the bobbin sleeve use a little graphite or easing oil.

Keep the driving band clean and renew it when frayed. Check that the cord attaching the treadle to the crankshaft or footman is of the correct length for comfortable treadling, and that the treadle just clears the ground when in its lowest position.

Spinning equipment
Baskets

Baskets or boxes are required for holding rolags etc. A shallow, flat-bottomed flower basket is suitable (figure 128).

Bath

A stainless steel, enamel, or galvanised bath is required for washing or scouring fleeces and skeins, and for dyeing.

Bobbins

Three or four bobbins are usually supplied with a spinning wheel. The bobbin (spool, pirn or quill) consists of a hollow stem onto which the yarn is spun, with a disc at one end (flat on the inside and domed on the outside to fit into the U shape of the flyer), and a grooved whorl at the other end (by which means the drive band turns the bobbin).

Bobbin rack

An upright rack (see figure 53) is required for holding bobbins when plying (see also *Lazy Kate*). This can be made from a wooden frame with rods pushed through corresponding holes drilled in the sides for suspending the bobbins. A rack is essential for plying unless the yarn has been wound into balls, or if the spinning wheel has two holders for spare bobbins (see figure 33) which allow them to rotate freely.

Bow

A cord attached to a bowed wooden stick is required for bowing (fluffing up) cotton fibre prior to carding (see figure 104). A bow can be made from a straight, strong but flexible branch of willow (or comparably suitable tree type). It should be between 2 and 3 ft (60 and 90 cm) long, and about $\frac{1}{2}$ in (1.2 cm) thick.

128 Shallow baskets are useful for containing rolags ready for spinning; keep all equipment which will be needed close to hand for ease of use

Attach a length of catgut (an old violin, cello or harp string will do), or a very smooth cord, to each end of the branch, bending it gently into a bow shape.

Breaker

A wooden mallet-type, or bladed-type, breaker is used for bruising flax prior to scutching.

Carders

A pair of carders is required for aligning the fibres of wool, cotton, and other materials in a particular direction to create a rolag for spinning. To be recommended are the wooden, curved back, leather clad, lightweight Scandinavian type. These are normally set with relatively fine wire hooks which are in the shape of a U; both ends protrude through the leather clothing, and have a forward bend about halfway along their length. ('Card clothing' is the term used to describe the wire hooks set in the leather, composition leather, or cotton webbing pad which covers the face of each carder.) The card clothing in the Scandinavian type is attached to the wooden base around the edges only, which allows for free movement of the hooks and obviates the breaking of the fibres in the carding process. Coarse wire hooks and an open sett are suitable only for very strong coarse fibres.

Ideally carders should be used by one person only. They should, from the outset, be labelled with an R (right hand carder) and L (left hand carder) respectively and kept to the same hands throughout their life (figure 129). Use separate pairs of carders for wool and cotton if possible.

129 A pair of Scandinavian carders

Clean the carders each time after use. This is especially important if they are to be used for a different type of fleece or other fibre, but it also helps to preserve them for a longer life, especially if oil and dirt are present. To do this, take one in each hand so that they are facing each other. Stroke the left hand carder down the right hand carder working towards the handle end, using a firm pecking motion repeated several times. Remove any fibres which are adhering. Repeat, using the right hand carder across the left hand carder. Raise all the fibres to the surface in this way, repeating the process until both carders are clean. Persistent clogging and dirty fibres may need to be lifted out by the use of a fine gauge knitting needle pushed down between the lines of hooks. It is a good idea to give an application of beeswax onto the back and handles of a new pair of carders before putting them to use.

Chair

A chair or stool of the correct height for the individual is essential for sitting at the spinning wheel comfortably, without tiring.

Clock reel

A clock reel, or yarn reel, is a windmill type skein winder which registers the yardage of the yarn wound onto it (see figure 67); it is therefore a valuable asset if large quantities are to be skeined. A simple ratchet system together with a dial records each 2 yd (2 m) length, and is operated by handle. A rotary reel is a variation on the design.

Cloth finishing roller

A large roller is required for wrapping woven cloth round for the wet finishing process. It may be made of long, thin wooden slats (see figure 67, and 'crabbing roller', page 83). It is also used for tentering cloth for drying.

Cover cloth

A plain, suitably coloured apron or cover should be laid across the lap when spinning to aid inspection of the thread (and keep one's clothes clean).

Distaff

A hand-held distaff is a long, narrow pole with a slight bulb at the top, which is held under the arm when spinning on a drop spindle (see figure 114). A spinning wheel distaff, used to hold the flax fibre, is a sturdy wooden pole which may be free-standing or attached to the spinning wheel. The top may be conical, lozenge or pear shaped (figure 118), or have a series of wooden protrusions up the stem.

Diz

Normally made of horn, this component of the woolcomber's tools is a small disc with a hole in it, which is used to control the formation of a top during jigging (see figure 50).

Dog comb

A dog comb is sometimes used to straighten locks of wool or fleece (a method used by Shetland spinners).

Dog stripping comb and clamp

This is a small comb which is clamped to a bench, through which wool fibre is pulled by hand for spinning worsted type yarn (see figure 32).

Drive band

The drive band circumvents the driving wheel and spindle whorl on a spinning wheel and causes the flyer to rotate round the bobbin (see figure 33). The size and type of cord to use is a matter of controversy, and also dependent on the width and shape of the pulley groove. Saddler's and shoemaker's linen twist is suitably fine and smooth, with little elasticity and very durable. Moreover it contains sufficient gripping power to prevent slippage, and is fine enough to allow for the use of a reef knot with a double turn without causing uneven rotation.

Hackling combs

Large combs with metal tines, made in a series of four or five from coarse through to fine, are used for aligning and refining flax fibres prior to spinning.

Lazy Kate

This is a type of bobbin rack used for plying (see figure 53).

Netting

Stain-proof (nylon) netting is useful for spreading fleeces out to dry.

Niddy noddy

This is a simple tool for winding skeins from the bobbin (see figure 66) and is normally designed to measure a length of 2 yd (2 m) of yarn at each turn. The central shaft has a crossbar at each end set at right angles to each other. The distance between the outer surface of these is 18 in (45 cm) for a 2 yd (2 m) skein circumference. This tool can easily be made, using a wooden shaft $\frac{3}{4}$ in (2 cm) square and 22 in (55 cm) long, and two lengths of wooden dowel $\frac{1}{2}$ in (1.2 cm) in diameter and 6 in (15 cm) long. Set one length of dowel in a drilled hole about 2 in (5 cm) from the top end of the shaft, and the other at right angles 2 in (5 cm) from the other end of the shaft, each protruding on either side and fixed with a strong adhesive. An extra allowance of about

1 in (2.5 cm) or more can be given in measuring the wood to allow for shrinkage of the yarn in washing, if required, or a meter measure can be used as an alternative.

Oil and oil can

Light machine oil or graphite grease is required for regular lubrication of the spinning wheel bearings.

Olive oil and atomizer

Olive oil, or a blend of olive oil, water and ammonia (ammonia acting as the emulsifier) in the ratio of $1:1:\frac{1}{2}$, is sometimes required for spraying on wool fibre before carding.

Revolving floor swift

A tall rack with revolving pulleys at top and bottom is required for holding mohair skeins taut while the surface is being raised with a brush (see figure 80).

Ribbon

A strong ribbon approximately $\frac{3}{4}$ in (2 cm) wide and 3 yd (3 m) long is used to bind flax onto the distaff.

Scales

These are sometimes needed for weighing whole fleeces. A spring-loaded, suspended type, having a large hook at the bottom, is ideal for hanging a bulky fleece. For smaller but bulky weighings of parts of fleece, hair fibres and stricks of flax, a large fulcrum balance with a good range of weights, from $\frac{1}{4}$ to 4 lb (100 g to 2 kg), and a generous sized pan is most satisfactory, and can often be procured second-hand. For very small quantities of chemical dyestuffs, smaller and more accurate scales are needed.

Scutching blade and board

The large wooden blade is used to beat retted flax against a board to remove the woody particles from the fibre bundles prior to hackling.

Skein rods and weights

A rod suspended from the ceiling (or a rack) is used to hold skeins of yarn for drying and setting. A second rod is passed through the bottom of the skeins, and a weight suspended from it to keep the skeins taut (see figure 67). Weights must not be too great, nor remain in place after the initial setting has been achieved.

Skein winder or skeiner

An umbrella type skein winder is invaluable for winding off yarn from washed skeins. A windmill type winder is an alternative to the niddy noddy (see also *clock reel*).

Spindle

1 The basic drop (suspended) spindle consists of a shaft, with a notch cut into one side near the top, and a whorl (consisting of a disc or crossed sticks) at the bottom (see figure 2). A simple spindle can be made from a piece of dowelling of pencil thickness about 10 in (25 cm) long, whittled at one end to a point and inserted into a hole in the centre of a wooden disc.

2 The spindle on a spindle wheel, like the drop spindle, acts as the 'bobbin' onto which the spun yarn is wound directly. An improvised spindle can be made from a heavy gauge knitting needle inserted in the orifice of a flyer wheel if a spindle wheel is not available.

3 The spindle on a flyer wheel is formed in one piece with the rotating flyer, and the bobbin is slipped onto it as a separate entity.

Teazle frame

A wooden frame mounted with dried teazle heads is used to raise the nap on wool and mohair fabrics (see figure 80).

Tensioning device

A tensioning device is sometimes required when plying. This can be made from a firm cardboard box approximately 9 by 20 in (22 by 50 cm), and 12 in (30 cm) high. Punch three or four pairs of holes (one each side of the

132 An Irish flax wheel showing the tall distaff attached to the stock of the spinning wheel

box), each pair at a different level from the others, e.g. the first 2 in (5 cm) from the top of the box, the second 6 in (15 cm) from the top, the third 2 in (5 cm) from the top, and the fourth (if required) at 6 in (15 cm). Push rods or long knitting needles through each pair of holes, and thread the singles yarns under and over these, using an opposite zigzag for each yarn (see figure 53).

Tentering frame

This is an adjustable wooden frame with a series of hooks along the top and bottom of its length for stretching fabric until dry. (See also *cloth finishing roller*.)

Threading hook

A threading hook to take the yarn through the orifice of the spinning wheel is easily made by straightening a paper clip and, using a pair of pliers, making a small hook-bend at one end, twisting a loop at the other end, then attaching

a 12 in (30 cm) length of string and tying it to the mother-of-all near the orifice side.

Tow fork

This is a type of distaff with three or four prongs rising from a platform at the top, used for holding tow flax for spinning.

Washing agents

Pure soap flakes or a solution from soft soap is safe for washing all wool and hair fibres. One or two detergents which are especially designed for wool (such as Lissapol N or Synperonic N, Teepol, Stergene) do not induce felting and are therefore easier to handle for scouring purposes if used in moderation.

Water pot

A bowl of water placed on a stool is required when wet spinning flax; some types of spinning wheel have a water pot built in. A solu-

tion made from pouring hot water onto
Carrageen Moss can be used instead of water.

Woolcomber's tools

These consist of a pair of hand combs, a pad and
a diz; a pan of hot water to heat the combs,
scales and a suitable table are also required.
Each comb consists of a row of long metal
tines set into a wooden handle (see figure
50).

Glossary of terms

Angora goat Animal producing Mohair.

Angora rabbit Longhaired breed of rabbit producing angora hair fibre.

Alpaca Related to camel and llama.

Bassinet Remaining silk of the inner part of the cocoon after reeling is completed – and of faulty cocoons.

Bast fibre Fibre from the stem of certain plants.

Bowing Whipping raw cotton by plucking catgut on a bow into a fibre mass.

Breaking Breaking up the rotted stem of the flax plant.

Britch Coarse fleece from the hind legs of a sheep.

Cabling Twisting together of two or more plied yarns.

Carding Creating a film of aligned fibres evenly dispersed.

Castle wheel An upright wheel having the spindle and flyer below the wheel.

Charka A spinning wheel used in India.

Clip A farmer's total yield of fleeces.

Coloured Natural brown and grey fleece as opposed to white or dyed fleece.

Combings Undercoat combed from various animals.

Count A number denoting thickness of yarn in a given yardage of a fixed weight. The higher the number the finer the yarn.

Crimp Natural kinks present along the length of a wool fibre.

Degumming Removal of natural gum from silk, by simmering in soap lather.

Denier A standard weight of a given length of filament yarn. In Britain, the weight in grams of 9000 metres of yarn; the higher the number, the thicker the yarn). This method of measurement originated in the silk industry.

Diamond Good quality part of a fleece from the back of a sheep.

Distaff A wooden upright pole designed to hold prepared flax from which to spin.

Doffing Method of removal of combed fibres from a wool comb.

Doubling Plying in twos.

Drafting Attenuation of a rolag or roving to produce a yarn.

Drafting zone The attenuated area between the two hands when drafting.

Dressed flax Flax prepared into flax 'line'.

Effect yarns Fancy, textured or multicoloured yarns.

Extra diamond Best quality part of a fleece from the sheep's shoulders and flanks.

Fibre mass Source of supply in the hand for spinning.

Filament Single continuous animal-formed thread (such as silk) or man-made thread (such as rayon).

Floss Fine filaments of silk which anchor the silkworm in position prior to it spinning its cocoon.

Flyer Horseshoe-shaped attachment to the spindle to guide the yarn onto the bobbin.

Flyer wheel Spinning wheel having a flyer complex.

Footman Crankshaft on treadle type spinning wheels.

Friction band Cord used to control spindle revolutions in relation to that of the bobbin.

Frisson Silk waste taken from the outer layer of the cocoon.

Gossip wheel Spinning wheel having twin spindles and flyers.

Grassing Bleaching of flax by exposure to sunlight and to oxygen from the grass on which it is laid.

Great wheel English name for Big Wheel.

Grey, in the Unscoured fabric containing oil and dirt.

Hackling Combing flax fibres.

Handle Textural feel.

Hemp A stem or bast fibre plant.

High wheel Big wheel (spindle wheel).

Hog fleece From first shearing of a yearling sheep.

Jute A stem or bast fibre.

Kemp Short hair fibres shed into the fleece. Resists dye.

Knops Small firm blobs of felted fibres integrated into the yarn.

Lantern Frame-type distaff head.

Line flax Fine hackled flax ready for spinning.

Llama Animal related to the camel family.

Lock Length (handful) of wool taken from the raw fleece.

Long wheel Irish name for Big Wheel.

Maidens   Two wooden uprights holding the spindle complex on a flyer wheel.

Matchings   Similar qualities of fleece from several like fleeces.

Mohair   Hair fibre from angora goat.

Moiety   The fine fleece from the head of a sheep.

Moorit   Warm, brown colour of Shetland fleece.

Mother-of-all   Complex on Flyer Wheel incorporating spindle, flyer, bobbin and maidens.

Noils   Short fibres remaining on woolcombs after preparation of tops. Silk noils are the short fibres left after combing.

Niddy noddy   Simple tool for winding skeins.

Orifice   Aperture on the metal spindle of the flyer wheel through which the yarn flows.

Pick fleece   Quality fleece in any class.

Picklock   Felted fleece from the belly of a sheep.

Plying   Twisting two, three or more singles yarns to form a thicker thread.

Prime   The rump area of a sheep's fleece.

Pulley   Grooved whorl on a wheel's spindle.

Pulling (flax)   Harvesting by pulling bundles of flax stems up with the roots.

Ramie   A stem or bast fibre plant.

Reeling   Winding off of a continuous filament of silk from a group of cocoons.

Retting   Soaking bundles of flax in water to create a bacterial action on the stem and core.

Rolag   A film of fibres aligned by carding and then rolled.

Roving   A fine continuous length of fibres prepared for spinning.

Saxony wheel   A flyer type two band wheel.

Semi-worsted   A loose term covering the spinning of wool (and hair fibres) other than a true woollen or true worsted.

Sericulture   Cultivation of silk from silkworms.

Scotch tensioner   A friction band used to control a single band treadle wheel. (See *friction band*.)

Scouring   Removal of dirt and grease by washing.

Scutching   Removal of the outer and inner woody part of a flax stem.

Singles   A single yarn produced by spinning raw or prepared fibre.

Skirtings   Excessively dirty, unusable parts of a fleece.

Sliver   Continuous rope of fibre without twist, ready for spinning.

Slub   A bulge in the yarn (usually at regular intervals).

Sorting   Dividing a fleece into different qualities.

Spindle   Shaft and whorl attachment.

Spinerette   Gland from which the silkworm exudes a solution. This solidifies in the air to form a thread.

Staple   Natural length of a lock of fleece.

Strick   A 'lock' of flax.

S twist   Anticlockwise direction of twist on a yarn.

Teasing   Separating the fibres in a lock of fleece.

Teazles   A cultivated variety of bristle-headed plants is used to raise the nap of a fabric.

Tension screw   A wooden screw controlling the movement of the mother-of-all, thus varying the tension of the drive bands.

Thread   Correctly means a plied yarn, also a singles silk filament.

Top   A continuous roving produced by woolcombing.

Tow   Coarse or broken flax fibres spun for rougher textures.

Twists per inch (TPI)   Number of twists in a yarn or thread along each inch.

Warp   Fixed threads running lengthwise on a woven fabric.

Weft   Filler yarn running across the woven fabric (woven in and out by means of a shuttle).

Whorl   Circular weight at the base of a hand spindle; also the pulley on a wheel driven spindle.

Woollen yarn   Spun from rolags using a long draft; an air-filled thread.

Worsted yarn   Spun from combed fibres using a short draft; a smooth thread.

Yarn   A collection of fibres twisted in a continuous length. Usually a singles.

Yarn size   Thickness, count. In Britain, USA and Australia, the number of ply is given first followed by the weight of the singles yarn. The weight is based on the number of hanks to the pound (the higher the number the thinner the yarn). The standard length of hank varies between 300 and 800 yards depending on the fibre. 3/6s would indicate a 3 ply yarn in which the singles yarn weighs 6 to the pound; 6s would indicate a singles yarn, unplied, weighing 6 hanks to the pound.

In Europe the standard hank length is 1000 metres for all fibres. The count indicates the number of hanks in 1 kg, and the number of ply is written after the singles count.

The international system Tex (not yet fully adopted) indicates the weight in grams of 1000 metres of yarn; the higher the number the thicker the yarn.

Z twist   Clockwise direction of twist on a yarn.

Bibliography

BAINES, Patricia, *Spinning Wheels*, Batsford, 1977,
Scribners 1978
BRONHOLM, HC, and HALD, Margrethe, *Costumes of
the Bronze Age in Denmark*, Nordisk Forlag, OUP
CHAPIN, Dolona, *Spinning Around the World:
International Hand Spinning Directory*, Fabius, NY,
1975
CHANNING, Marion, *Textiles Tools of Colonial
Homes*, 1971
CROWFOOT, Grace and LING ROTH, H, *Hand Spinning
and Woolcombing*, R Bean 1974
DAVENPORT, Elsie, *Your Hand Spinning*, Sylvan
Press
ELLACOTT S E, *Spinning and Weaving*, 1956
FANNIN, Allen, *Hand Spinning: Art and Technique*,
Van Nostrand Reinhold 1970
GRASSETT, *Complete Guide to Hand Spinning*
HOCHBERG, Bette, *Handspinner's Handbook*
LEADBEATER, Eliza, *Hand Spinning*, Studio Vista
1976
McLEOD, Ella, *Why Spin* (leaflet)
TEAL, Peter, *Hand Woolcombing and Spinning: A
Guide to Worsteds*, Blandford 1976
WEIR, Sheilagh, *Spinning and Weaving in Palestine*,
British Museum 1970

Other publications
CIBA REVIEW, *The Spinning Wheel*, 1939, reprint
1977
THOMPSON, G B (Ed.), *Spinning Wheels: Horner
Collection*, Ulster Museum, Belfast
British Sheep Breeds: Their Wools and Uses, British
Wool Marketing Board
GILBERT, K R, *Textile Machinery*, Science Museum
1970

List of suppliers

Sources of supplies change from time to time. Many new names are added to the lists as the demand for equipment increases and a few cease to be makers or agents for these appliances. The following list includes only a fractional number of suppliers, and it is advisable to contact one of the national authorities to ascertain addresses of local suppliers. In Britain, Canada and the United States, suppliers import stocks of wheels, carders and other equipment from Norway, Denmark, New Zealand and several other countries.

Great Britain
Equipment

Camden Weavers
16 Lower High Street
Chipping Camden, Glos.

Susan Foster
9 Windemere Road
Kendal, Cumbria

Handweavers Studio
29 Haroldstone Road
London E17 7AN

Frank Herring
27 Higher West Street
Dorchester, Dorset

Kennet Woolshop
77 High Street
Marlborough, Wiltshire SN8 1HF

Eliza Leadbeater
Rookery Cottage
Dalesfords Lane, Whitegate,
Northwich, Cheshire

Jim Williamson
Timber Top Tables Co.
159 Main Street
Asfordby
Melton Mowbray
Leicestershire
LE14 3TS

T J Willcocks
Hedgehog Equipment
Forest Craft Centre
Upper Hartfield, East Sussex

Fleeces

British Wool Marketing Board
Kew Bridge House
Brentford
Middlesex TW8 0EL

Cotswold Farm Park
Bemborough
Guiting Power, Glos

Hedgehog Equipment (address above)

Jacob Fleece Society
Sec. Mrs John Thornley
St Leonards
Tring, Herts

Eliza Leadbeater (address above)

Local Wool Staplers

Craftsman's Mark Ltd
(Wool Matchings)
Trefnant
Denbigh, Clwyd

Hair fibres

Cottage Crafts
1 Aked Street
Bradford

Eliza Leadbeater (address above)

Flax and raw cotton

Eliza Leadbeater (address above)

Information

Animal Breeding Research Organisation
Field Laboratory
Roslin
Midlothian
Scotland

Association of Guilds of Weavers, Spinners and
Dyers
c/o Five Bays
10 Stancliffe Avenue
Marford, Wrexham, Clwyd

British Wool Marketing Board
Oak Mills, Station Road
Clayton
Bradford
West Yorkshire

CoSIRA
35 Wimbledon Common
London SW19

Crafts Advisory Committee
28 Haymarket
London SW1

Federation of British Craft Societies
British Craft Centre
43 Earlham Street
London WC2

London Guild of Weavers, Spinners and Dyers
c/o 80 Scotts Lane
Bromley
Kent

USA

International Handspinning Directory
Mrs Kenneth Chapin
2178 Pompey-Fabius Road
RD 1 Fabius
New York

Shuttle, Spindle and Dyepot
1013 Farmington Avenue
West Hertford
Conn 06107

Handweavers' Guild of America Inc
65 La Salle Road
West Hartford
Conn 06107

The following magazines give information on
equipment and materials.

The Weaver's Journal
The Colorado Fiber Center
P.O. Box 2049
Boulder
Colorado 80306

Fiberarts
50 College Street
Asheville
North Carolina 28801

Interweave
2938 North Country Road
Loveland
Colorado 80537

Australia

Crafts Council of A.C.T.
Canberra Spinners and Weavers
Crafts Council of New South Wales
Handweavers and Spinners Guild of Australia
Crafts Council of Queensland
Queensland Spinners Weavers and Dyers Group
Crafts Council of South Australia
Handweavers and Spinners Guild of S.A.
Crafts Council of Tasmania
Handweavers Spinners and Dyers Guild of Tasmania
Crafts Council of Victoria
Handweavers and Spinners Guild of Victoria
Crafts Council of Western Australia
Handweavers and Spinners Guild of W.A.
Crafts Council of Australia, Sydney

Index

Craft plays an important role in the Kingdom of Beauty of the world: its products have a close relationship with the daily life of common people.

From *The Unknown Craftsman* by Seotsu Yanagi

The Craft of
HAND SPINNING

Hand spinning of wool and fibres is one of the oldest and most basic of crafts, and every aspect is covered in this thoroughly practical book. Beginning with the choice of fleece, the preparation, spindle and wheel spinning and how to produce different yarns, it then discusses spinning with animal and vegetable fibres and the various techniques that are required. A final section is a review of the development of spinning techniques through the ages and advice on buying a spinning wheel and making simple tools and equipment.

168 pages   130 black and white photographs
1 line illustration   5 colour photographs

BATSFORD
net price
£3·95

A BATSFORD CRAFT PAPERBACK

ISBN 0 7134 1012 4